THE
MAXIMALIST

THE MAXIMALIST

COLORFUL INTERIORS FOR BOLD LIVING

DANI DAZEY

ABRAMS, NEW YORK

1/ LIVE

2/ STAY

3/ WORK

INTRODUCTION

Life is colorful. I believe your home should be too. If you've picked up this book, it's likely you agree. I have no formal training as an interior designer, but I've spent the last eight years creating spaces that make people happy—rooms bursting with color, pattern, and soul. I want to show you how to do the same in your home because I believe it will enhance every aspect of your life.

The child of creatives, I grew up in a house with a raspberry-colored kitchen, which probably tells you a lot about where I gained my color confidence. I was the type of kid who loved anything artistic: I sewed clothes for my dolls and redecorated my room a zillion times. As a teen, I was obsessed with designing homes on Sims.

By the time I hit college, I felt like I needed to pick a professional lane, so I chose fashion design. I spent the early years of my career designing graphics for big apparel brands, but when I landed at a start-up, it opened my eyes to creative entrepreneurship. Soon after, I used my savings to launch my own clothing line, Dazey LA.

As I built Dazey LA's brand online, I shared everything about creating the business. As the face of the brand, I posted everyday things like how I was decorating and what I was painting in my free time. The spaces I designed really resonated with my audience, and I slowly realized that I could create clothes and art *and* interiors. I didn't have to be boxed into just one thing—and in fact,

working as a multi-hyphenate has made me even more creative. Being self-taught in interiors with a background in fashion has also given me more freedom than your average interior designer.

My vivid interior style runs counter to some of the trends in recent years, but I know it's captured many people's hearts from the messages I receive. I understand why minimalism, modern farmhouse, and quiet luxury are popular. A neutral palette is an easy way to furnish your home: Everything will match and nothing will offend. But I'm not interested in anything quiet. I want a lively life, a happy home, and rooms that make my heart sing every time I walk into them. Don't you?

When I see homes with white walls and beige sofas, I wonder "Who lives here? What are they like?" If you walk into one of the interiors I've designed, you'll know a lot about who resides there before you even meet the homeowner. You'll find art and objects that draw you in and colors that speak to that particular individual—not some imagined future buyer scouring Zillow. Our homes are where life unfolds. They should offer a narrative of who we are and what we like, and I doubt anyone's story is a boring white box.

Our homes are not just a reflection of who we are; they also have the power to influence who we will become. I've always been fascinated by how environments (and design, in general) can affect people. You can put on a bold outfit that you love, then walk out of your house feeling confident, ready for anything. The same is true of interiors. The colors and objects you choose to surround yourself with impact your mood and outlook; a room can leave you feeling inspired, uplifted, or soothed.

I want to empower you to tell your own story in your home. What lights you up? What do you want to look at first thing every day? What have you secretly always admired but been afraid to try yourself? What color dominates your pinboards?

People often tell me that living in a home as saturated as my own would be "overwhelming," but I can tell you that inhabiting a colorful house isn't chaotic. To me, it's energizing and creatively nourishing. Others dismiss my happy, maximalist style as "juvenile," but that doesn't bother me: Children are born with an innate understanding that color is positive (it's literally a signal of an abundance of resources in nature). Meanwhile, most of the adults I know seem almost like they are afraid of color, and because they're all so concerned with having "good taste," sophistication, or worst of all, "resale value," they've shut joy out of their homes.

When you decorate your home with things that you love, it's an act of creative self-expression. When you embrace self-expression, it's empowering in so many more ways than just aesthetic fulfillment: It bleeds into all the other areas of your life.

This book will be your guide to looking at your own home with new eyes as I take you on tours of more than a dozen interiors that I have designed. I'll walk you through the rooms of my own homes and the spaces I've designed for clients and tell you exactly what I did—and why.

These aren't meant to be picture-perfect interiors; rather they are spaces of exploration and celebration that reflect the people that live, stay, and work in them. Throughout the book, I've highlighted what I'm calling "Dazey DIYs," little projects that I did with a minimum of time and effort—ones that I hope will inspire your own creativity. At the end of each home tour, I've also pulled out tips and tricks to connect the dots between what you see in these pages and how it relates to your own home. And finally, at the back of the book, I've spilled all the details on my favorite sources—the brands, shops, and resources that have helped me create my signature Dazey look. I've shared everything from my very first personal projects to no-expenses-spared client work because design is a constant evolution. I want to show you that your home can grow and change *with* you—in fact, that's what makes it fun. Bright, playful design is for everyone, whether you live in a modest space or a mansion.

My Color Theory

Did you know our world is getting less colorful? When The Science Museum Group analyzed photos of everyday objects, they determined that our possessions were becoming less and less colorful over time, and the story went viral (and kept going viral for years as new people shared it). This study confirmed what most of us have already observed: Our world is losing saturation, charm, and uniqueness as design becomes more homogenized. I believe that study got so much buzz because deep down, we know color is important.

I say we should fight back against this trend. Let's stop living in boring black and white! We all grew up loving colors, so why are we so afraid of them now? Creating colorful spaces has brought me so much joy and is the ultimate form of self-expression. Here's what I know about designing with color:

THERE ARE NO BAD COLORS

I believe that there are no unlovable hues and no color is "ugly." Seriously, there are no bad colors! Every color can sing somewhere, and almost any combination of hues can work if you fine-tune the ratios, shades, and tints.

USE HUES THAT MAKE YOU SMILE

A good color scheme starts with a particular shade you love. Take that one hue and build from there, experimenting until it feels right to you. Use your intuition. You might be surprised with where the process takes you.

TREAT THE COLOR WHEEL LIKE A COMPASS

The color wheel is a useful tool: It can point you in the right direction for your color palette, but it's not a map. My palettes often use principles derived from the color wheel, like complementary colors (those opposite one another on the wheel), but usually with a twist: Instead of straight green and red, I'll pair a minty green with pink, which is a tint of red.

COLORS ARE ALWAYS IN CONVERSATION

The celebrated decorator David Hicks once said, "Colors do not clash: They vibrate." And it's true: Colors feel different when they are placed next to one another. Complementary colors, for example, usually accentuate one another. A shade of purple can look neutral when placed next to a bright, zippy orange, but look positively plum when cast against pure white.

CONSISTENCY ALLOWS FOR PLAYFULNESS

As my design practice has taken me into more complex color combinations, I have learned that you can get away with a greater variety of hues in a single room, if you are consistent with the ones you use. This is why it makes sense to match paint precisely to wallpaper and to go the extra mile to find accessories in your chosen palette. If you have a bunch of similar-but-not-quite-matching shades of a color, it can be confusing to the eye.

7 Dazey Design Principles

While I don't believe in rules when it comes to decorating, I *do* have some design truths that have solidified over the years. Consider them a blueprint for finding your style.

1. DECORATING SHOULD BE FUN

Seriously, guys: This should be joyful—not stressful. Making your home your own should make you smile and light you up. If you're scared to get things "wrong," try to remember that paint and throw pillows can easily be changed. The stakes are low, and the rewards are high.

2. HOMES SHOULD BE PERSONAL

Your interiors should be designed to bring *you* pleasure—not someone else. They should be filled with more than a few of your favorite things—a fridge covered in silly snapshots, a painting found on your travels, or your grandma's "good" dishes; these personal touches are what makes a house a home. Increasingly, homes are decorated to be appealing to the masses and not made for the people living in them, and I find that sad!

3. DESIGN MATTERS

Decorating is a form of self-expression, and a big goal of mine is to empower people to embrace the things that they love. I know so many people who admire bright colors and playful design, but they get terrified when it comes to applying that to their space. When you can finally embrace that self-expression in your home, it is liberating in so many more ways than just aesthetics. Interior design is not frivolous: It impacts your attitude and mindset and flows into all the other areas of your life.

4. NOTHING IS TIMELESS

Take a look at any style from decades past and it's sure to look dated, even if it was billed as "classic" or "timeless" at the time (hello, Tuscan-style kitchen of the '00s). I believe you should design a space you love in the here and now, not one that you think will still appeal to someone else at a future date. Fashions come and go faster than ever, and there is really no such thing as a timeless design. So, I say you might as well go with your gut because you're probably going to like that longer than whatever is considered "timeless" at the moment.

5. FUNCTION AND BEAUTY GO HAND IN HAND

It often feels like the design world is divided between practical, space-planning advice and purely style-driven content, but beauty and function must always work together. Smart space planning makes for rooms that look and feel good. Thoughtful storage lets you live your life more comfortably and keeps the clutter out of your carefully designed rooms. Function and beauty—you really can't have one without the other.

6. LABELS AREN'T ALWAYS HELPFUL

TikTok and Instagram love a hyper-specific microtrend—think "grandmillenial" or "quiet luxury"—but I don't think those labels are useful for finding your personal style. I am a "maximalist"

when it comes to pattern and color, but a "minimalist" when it comes to actual stuff (look at any of my designs and you'll see the bare minimum of clutter). Use those catchy decor names to help you search for inspiration, but never feel like you should decorate to fit the definition of a particular style.

7. YOU'RE NEVER DONE DECORATING

I bought my first home seven years ago, and it's still not "finished." I don't think any home ever is. Life happens, your needs change, and in turn your home will too. You and your home are having a conversation: Keep it lively.

1/

LIVE

MY PRETTY-IN-PINK PENTHOUSE

This massive rental let me stretch my design skills and helped me build my confidence with color.

Our Beachwood Canyon apartment was the first Los Angeles apartment where my then-boyfriend, now-husband, Phillip, and I got to start fresh with the decor as a couple. This sprawling three-bedroom was such a cool spot: The living room had these super-high beamed ceilings, a vintage fireplace, and gorgeous original floors. It was also in a magical location right underneath the Hollywood sign in the hills. We scored a killer deal because the landlord had no photos online. It really felt like we'd won the housing lottery.

We were excited to make the space our own, and our landlord said we were free to paint: His only stipulation was no wallpaper. You might be surprised to hear that the first step I took was to give everything a coat of white paint, but the walls were all a dingy beige that had to go. Then, I set out to convince Phillip that we should go all-in on pink, and as you'll see: He (mostly) agreed.

Because I'd always been a renter, I was still getting comfortable being daring with color. (Our Dazey Desert House on page 149 was a work in progress at that time too.) One way I began to explore was by giving each room a strong, single-color theme. I also relied more on accent walls and pops of hues than I would today. I'd dabbled in colorful upholstered furniture before, but this apartment was the point of no return.

Looking back, I can see that this home was a stepping stone on my path to gaining my color confidence: I was experimenting and growing. The lessons I learned decorating this home allowed me to really embrace maximalism in my future spaces.

DAZEY DIY

Make your own art. When I needed something for the wall in this room, I ordered frames and made portraits of me and Phillip to fit them. I used the technique of drawing the whole image without once lifting up my pen.

opposite

The living room's original tiled fireplace inspired the pink-and-green palette and led me to this a-*mazing* vintage Moroccan rug and floor pillows. The rug grounded the color scheme and pulled the whole room together.

right

The office has its own vibe, but the green accent wall and velvet upholstery are the same paint and fabric used in the living space.

DAZEY DIY

Style your shelves. First, split your book collection up and arrange them to create little rainbow moments on each shelf. Then add accessories that reinforce your color theme, arranging them so that everything feels evenly distributed. Aim for a variety of materials and textures.

I saw the apartment's built-in shelves as an opportunity to add pops of color without having to paint a whole wall. They also act as a visual balance to other elements in the room and help spread color around the room.

IN PRAISE OF COLORFUL COUCHES!

One thing you'll notice throughout our Beachwood Canyon home is that every piece of upholstered furniture is a vivid velvet. I encourage you to embrace color in your upholstery choices. Sure, a beige sofa will match with everything, but I'm sorry, it's just no fun! When we decided to go for one big statement couch, it transformed this room—our friends are still talking about this couch! Trust me: A bold sofa might feel too stimulating upon first consideration, but as you live with it, the impact of the color will mellow out and feel just right.

left/below

The kitchen's blush tile floors were practically begging me to paint the walls pink to match; plus, this room is open to the living and dining rooms, so it made sense to just keep the color theme going. If you've got uninspired white cabinets, painting the walls puts you on a fast track to personality.

A new, three-globe light fixture transformed this space both stylistically and practically: It's nice to have some light over your work area!

opposite

Uncharacteristically, I decided to keep the dining area white because the coved ceiling made it hard to paint without doing the ceilings *and* the walls. Opting for barrel-style dining chairs let me bring in color in another way (they were also extra comfy for working from home).

above

As an entrepreneur, I use my homes as shoot locations, so I'm always trying to sneak in an extra backdrop for photos. Looking into this corner, you can see how having two distinct accent walls that relate to each other helps the room feels cohesive. Fun, right?

opposite

This little room was my creative sanctuary, and therefore a great candidate for a full gallery wall treatment complete with my grandmother's artwork. I included a wall hanging and some painted canvas pieces to break up all the rigid lines. Mixing more tactile pieces in with framed art always, *always* makes a gallery wall more interesting. See page 155 for all my gallery wall tips.

Amplify your headboard. A painted color block behind a statement headboard makes an even louder statement. I created a circle sized to match my "french fry" bed (it's meant to look like the sun!), but you could do any shape that inspires you.

opposite

Behold the famous "french fry" bed, a nickname my Instagram followers bestowed on this channeled beauty. Silly names aside, statement furniture is an A+ way to make a space feel super bold without altering the room itself.

right

Our daylight-drenched bedroom was a natural fit for sunny accents. Painting all four walls would have cast too much of a yellow tint, but pops of lemon, including the built-in bookcase, paired with crisp white, shades of orange, and lots of leafy plants created such a lively, happy space.

MY PRETTY-IN-PINK PENTHOUSE
TIPS & TRICKS

Start with a clean slate

Why building owners favor shades of Band-Aid and beige instead of plain, clean white is beyond me. If you move into a place that has a funky neutral on the walls, it's definitely worth it to paint everything pure white for a fresh foundation to layer color onto.

Begin with just one color

Sticking to one main color per room is an ideal entry-level way to explore color. Start with a single color, then vary the tones, and once you're feeling confident pick your accent hue. Today I'm working with more complex color schemes and enjoying the challenge, but I had to work my way up to that.

Add an accent wall

I just *love* an accent wall. You'll see many of them in the pages to come. If you're just getting started with your design journey, I say update just one wall. If you use paint or peel-and-stick wallpaper it's a relatively low-cost and low-commitment way to bring color or pattern into your home, and I bet it'll make you want more.

Listen to your space

Sometimes you have to let the space choose the color palette. In this house the existing tiles influenced my color choices in the living room, kitchen, and bathroom. Likewise, we opted for sconces that felt like they were right for the era of the architecture.

Paint selectively

We didn't want it to be a big pain to bring this rental back to baseline when we moved out, so we painted accents and a lot of little built-in areas. If you're not ready for a big commitment, look for a discrete element you can paint, like a single wall, trim, a threshold, or a window well.

Seek out secondhand rugs

I'm a huge fan of vintage Moroccan rugs because they're so vibrant and handmade. Plus, the abstract designs are imperfect in a playful, artsy way that I love. You can find them through online dealers and Etsy, but it's especially fun to shop for them in person, if you can. Another huge plus? Since they're pre-loved they barely shed at all.

Say yes to velvet

Velvet is gorgeous, soft, and available in oh-so-many rich colors, but a lot of people avoid it because they assume velvet is a fussy fabric that will get dirty fast. It's not true! Most velvet upholstery is polyester (which, PS, is plastic) and wildly resilient: We had our two dogs run all over this light pink couch and I just wiped it clean with a little cleanser and a cloth. So don't fear velvet.

I persuaded my landlord to let us paint the inner wall of our patio in a fun shade of bubblegum. A little color, plus Bend Goods furniture, and a few sculptural cactuses made such a difference in this small space.

MY CALIFORNIA BUNGALOW GONE WILD

After years of holding back my style in rentals, I had so much fun decorating my first owned home in Los Angeles. This space is saturated with color and personality, from the front steps down to the closet doors.

I had been longing to buy a home in Los Angeles for years, but I almost didn't go to see this house because it didn't look like anything special in the listing photos. However, from the moment I stepped inside, I knew it was "the one."

The 1920s, Spanish-style house had a great layout and some sweet bungalow charm (hello, cove ceilings!), plus it had cool front and back yards. Outside it was painted what I call "grown" (aka, gray-brown) and it was super minimal on the interior. But this is exactly what I like: A blank slate—something I can take from an all-white box to a really funky space.

At just 1,200 square feet, it's modest in size, but that didn't prevent me from decorating it in a maximalist way. People have this misconception that color and pattern make rooms seem smaller, but this house is proof that they can make a space feel bigger and more grand.

Outside, we made the most of every square foot—this is California real estate, after all! We regraded the property to make the front yard more usable, added a stock tank pool, expanded a deck, and created an outdoor living room. Then I dressed everything with sweet and mellow shades of shell and mint—major vacay vibes.

Inside and out, there is so much more for your eyes to look at. People walk into this house and they are blown away and delighted by it. I smile every time I walk up to it too: I always wanted to own a pink home.

I always pay special attention to the first thing you see when you enter a room. In this house, the fireplace wall is where your eye lands, so I painted it a sunshine-y shade of yellow. The fireplace became an attention grabber thanks to the Fireclay tile. The scalloped Hygge & West wallpaper overhead draws your eye toward the focal point wall.

opposite

I left the dining room walls mostly white, but brought in color with hand-painted supergraphics (love me a pop of orange) and a soft shade of blush on the ceiling. The chunky rug anchors the space and layers in rich eggplant to give the palette depth. Notice how the caning repeats on the chairs and the sideboard.

above/left

The galley-style kitchen was a model of efficiency, but it was *b-o-r-i-n-g*. I painted the existing cabinets a lively lime and swapped the hardware—two kitchen refreshes that anyone can do. More significantly, we ripped out the gray slab counters and replaced them with hand-painted ceramic tiles. We also ditched the outdated appliances and light fixtures. You'll discover I have a personal vendetta against recessed can lights.

DAZEY DIY

I love to create a painted accent on the ceiling around a pendant lamp. It's so much easier than a whole ceiling mural and harkens back to the ceiling medallions you'd find on old, plastered ceilings.

opposite

This addition was being used as the primary bedroom, but it had nice access to the patio, so I converted it to a den. To make the addition feel more like the rest of the 1920s house, I added trim and wallpaper to the ceiling and swapped out the can lighting for cool, semiflush fixtures. But I didn't want it to feel *too* traditional (obvi!), so I opted for an acid-green sectional and walls to counteract that traditional element.

right

The bungalow has a small outbuilding that we use as an office and creative space. Because it was detached from the house, I felt extra free decorating it and went for a statement-y wall mural. It's the ultimate Zoom backdrop and so on-brand for me! My callers can't see the floor, but I love the look of layered rugs.

DAZEY DIY

Instead of replacing these louvered closet doors, I painted them in the four main colors used in the room, turning them into a fun feature.

left

I chose the smallest bedroom in the house for our bedroom, since we spend most of our time just sleeping there. This room is also my first twist on the traditional single-pattern room, but in a contemporary botanical pattern from Hygge & West instead of a fussy, old-fashioned floral.

opposite

The original bathroom was what most people look for: an all-white space. But not me—I craved color. Having a pink, unapologetically feminine bathroom was my ultimate dream, so when we renovated I went for it. The room reads maximalist, but take that wallpaper down and it would be quite understated. Peep how the classic checkerboard tiles not only alternate between pink and white, but also between shiny and matte.

opposite

Small outdoor spaces are often neglected dumping grounds, but I knew this narrow space between the house and the outbuilding could be a room of its own. The patio umbrella creates a "ceiling" for the room. I even painted a supergraphic onto the backside of the neighbor's privacy fence (shhhh, don't tell!).

above

It's amazing what a difference a coat of minty fresh paint made to the deck and railings, which were all painted bleh-brown. This part of the yard was basically a rocky dirt patch, so we turfed it to make it usable: It's one of those small improvements that made a big impact.

left

The little deck coming off the bedroom was closed off, so we opened it up and Phillip rebuilt the deck for the cowboy plunge pool. When people see my work, they see color and pattern, but creating better flow and maximum function is the foundation of every space.

DON'T FORGET THE FIFTH WALL

In most homes, the ceiling gets no attention at all (in fact, many people don't even bother to give it a fresh coat of paint!). I believe that the ceiling is begging to be decorated. By adding color or pattern to the ceiling, you automatically create an element of surprise: People aren't used to an artful ceiling. It's also a place where you can try a color or wallpaper that you might not want on all four walls. Here are a few ways you might decorate your ceilings:

ACCENT

If you have a white-walled room that could use a little more saturation (and you can always use more color!), why not paint the ceiling in a hue that is found in the room's decor? Just like an accent wall, an accent ceiling gives the room a strong design element and also helps tie the room together for a more finished look.

LACQUERED

Take an accent ceiling and dial up the drama with high-gloss paint. Using a super-shiny finish on the ceiling reflects light around the room and adds some glamor. Do note that this will look best on a smooth, blemish-free ceiling surface.

TONAL

If a full-on accent ceiling feels too bold, try a tonal ceiling hue. This could be a tint of white, like the very palest pink or blue, or it could be a tint of the wall color, say a peach ceiling with a tangerine wall.

COLOR DRENCH

Color drenching is when you paint *everything* in a room—walls, ceiling, trim, doors—in one color. The effect is dramatic and cocooning. If you've got a small room, I believe painting the ceiling the same color as the walls can make the room feel more expansive.

WALLPAPERED

I *adore* wallpaper on the ceiling: It's unexpected and playful in the best possible way. Plus, it's way less of an investment to wallpaper the ceiling than a whole room. One word of caution: Wallpapering the ceiling is tricky, so you may want to call in a pro installer.

MURAL

A ceiling mural has much the same effect as a wall mural, lending a room an arty looseness that I love. Sometimes a wall mural naturally wants to continue onto the ceiling and other times, I paint a mural just on the ceiling.

PAINTED MEDALLION

Perhaps the easiest DIY project for the ceiling is to paint a small design around a pendant light. Think of this as a low-cost, modern take on the traditional ceiling medallion. I've painted and stenciled organic squiggles and daisies around light fixtures for a little playful punch (see more on pages 89 and 239).

MY CALIFORNIA BUNGALOW GONE WILD

TIPS & TRICKS

Use your space your way

Think outside of the box when it comes to how you're going to use rooms. We turned the main bedroom into a second living room. You might give your kids the biggest bedroom or jettison the guest bedroom's bed and make it a workout space instead.

Can we talk about pink?

You may have surmised that I love, love, *love* pink, but the color can be controversial. Still considered a "girly" color, pink can be a hard sell with some men, while others disparage it as "over" after the long-enduring trend of "millennial pink." To me, blush is almost like a neutral. It is such a calming, peaceful color and it ties in well with so many other hues. If you're longing to add pink to your own home, don't let anyone tell you not to.

Let it be

We've all heard the phrase "If it ain't broke, don't fix it," but too often I see people ripping out perfectly functional kitchens in an effort to get the exact look they desire. This house had a relatively new kitchen with quality cabinets. They might not have been precisely what I would have chosen, but it was more sustainable (for both my budget and the planet) to paint the old ones than to start over.

Tile counters deserve a second chance

Tile is such an underrated surface, and it is a great way to bring pattern and color into more than just the bathroom. People have basically abandoned using tile in the kitchen, but we love our tiled kitchen counters, which felt right for our Spanish-style home. Tile cleans up easily, and I went with a darker grout, so we don't have to worry about it looking dirty. Everyone just uses a plain slab these days, but I am here to champion the lost art of tiled counters.

A little bit of black

Repeat after me: Every room needs contrast! The living and dining rooms are a great example of the power of black accents. Flip back and imagine those rooms with white accents in place of the black: It would change the whole feeling of the space. Adding just a touch of ebony gives a room definition and a subtle edge—and it's so easy to try!

The magic of moldings

The bungalow's cove ceilings inspired me to play with molding and trim for the first time. One molding trick that even the most beginner DIYer can try is adding a chair rail to a room. All you need is a handsaw and a miter box to cut the corners and a hammer, level, and finishing nails to hang it up. Of course, you can also hire a handyman if you don't want to do it yourself.

A COTTAGECORE CELEBRATION OF GIRLHOOD

With a little innovative design, this basic rental became a true reflection of my client. This project proves that home decor can be both an act of self-expression and self-preservation.

I was so thrilled when actress and social media star Dylan Mulvaney asked me to help her decorate her Los Angeles cottage. Dylan wanted something a little different from my usual look—a more cottage-inspired style with a serene vibe. I was excited to flex in a new direction, and it was a particularly fun challenge because this was a rental where we couldn't make any major changes. Paint, furnishings, and textiles would have to do the bulk of the work.

We drew inspiration from so many sources for this project, but especially from some of Dylan's favorite fictional places: Mrs. Honey's house in *Matilda* and Eloise's suite at the Plaza Hotel. In a way, decorating this cottage was like reclaiming the child-hood bedroom that Dylan wished she could have had growing up. We created the dream space she never got to experience.

The kitchen and bath were particularly tricky because we couldn't replace any of the humdrum cabinets, counters, and tile. With a little creativity and the help of some handy peel-and-stick products, I transformed both spaces for Dylan.

This rental shows that you can (and should!) make your home into a personal retreat—even if you are just renting. It's also a great example of how personalizing the place where you live can be both a form of self-expression and a way to create a comforting oasis from the world.

When designing a gallery wall, my trick is to lay it out on the floor first. Get the arrangement perfect, and then take a photo, so you can match that on the wall.

opposite

Isn't this bedroom sweet? Dylan wanted her sleeping space to be a place she could relax and feel at peace. She didn't want to paint the walls, so I added the color through textiles, including the pink and white gingham drapes. In this windowed corner, the curtains create an effect almost like wallpaper.

right

Dylan had the idea to create what we called "The Woman Wall," a montage of women she finds inspiring. To execute it in a way it would be cohesive with the rest of the room, I printed photos of the ladies in black and white, and framed them all in pink frames. You could do a similar project on just about any theme.

left

The key to maximalist style is maximum coordination. Notice how I stuck to a tight palette of pink, yellow, and white, with dashes of dark gray in the rug. The checkerboard print ties back to the rest of the house, and the wallpaper, rug, and throw pillows all relate to one another with their organic, fanning shapes.

opposite

A little vintage goes a long way: The gingham chair and antique light give the room instant character. Granny-style curtains were a renter-friendly way to achieve the cottagecore aesthetic Dylan desired. These curtains perfectly hit that cottage note— without feeling *too* grandma.

opposite

This bathroom! Y'all, even I was amazed by how it turned out: We used a stick-on tile from Mirth Studio to cover up the boring gray tile. On the walls, candy-striped wallpaper and images pulled from the pages of *Eloise at the Plaza* created the feminine bathroom Dylan was dreaming of—and we didn't have to change a single fixed element. A favorite detail: The tiered cake stand filled with bath bombs shaped like macarons!

above/left

Not gonna lie: This kitchen was a challenge. I am including it to encourage you to make your rental kitchen your own. The trick here was ordering a wallpaper with custom colors that incorporated the existing gray and black elements with Dylan's preferred pink. To refresh the recessed can lights, I created a daisy-shaped stencil and painted around each light.

I transformed this awkward corner into a breakfast nook with some precision shopping. This bench fits the corner so well it almost looks built in.

A COTTAGECORE CELEBRATION OF GIRLHOOD
TIPS & TRICKS

Work with what you've got

In a rental (and even in an owned home), there will be colors in the fixed elements you can't avoid. Rather than ignore them, I try to weave them into my color scheme. For example, there were gray elements in the primary bathroom that we couldn't change, so I incorporated gray, a color I normally tend to avoid, into the primary bedroom through the rug, pillow piping, and the grayscale of the photos.

Build in meaning

There are so many ways you can build meaning into a home. In Dylan's cottage, the trans pride flag inspired the palette for the living room. Other people probably won't get that connection right away, but it's a subtle way to celebrate her in her home.

Go semicustom

Dylan wanted a big, comfortable couch, but her living room was small, so we ended up ordering just two pieces of what would normally be a three-piece sofa. It was a great way to get that cozy sectional chaise piece without having to order a fully custom sofa.

Fake some trim

Molding gives a room architectural interest, but adding it to a rental isn't practical, so I gave this cottage ceiling my "trick trim" with paint. It's literally just two colorful lines painted around the ceiling, but it tricks the eye into thinking there's some detail there.

Fake a pendant

Another lighting trick for rentals is to buy corded fixtures like the cool vintage light in Dylan's reading corner. All you need to do to add this type of lighting is screw in a hook above where you want the light to hang, rig the cord over the hook, and plug it in.

Upgrade your overheads

In a rental it can feel like you're stuck with the landlord's ugly light fixtures, but I encourage renters to buy and install lights they love. You just need to save and store the original lighting, so you can put it back before you leave. If you're not comfortable installing a light yourself, hire a handyman to do it for you.

Broaden your shopping horizons

When you're decorating, don't just look to your usual favorite stores. You can find unique things in unexpected places; for example, I searched for floral curtains with valances and went down the rabbit hole of a bunch of decidedly uncool retailers to find them.

A BOHO-DECO MASH-UP

Drawing inspiration from an eclectic mix of eras, I packed a ton of personality into my client's formerly builder-grade space.

This living and dining space was one of my very first projects for a client. The house had a choice location and an airy atmosphere, but when my client bought it, all the character had been renovated out of it. We're talking zero charm. It felt run-of-the-mill, and my client was anything but generic. So, she asked me to bring personality back to the home's main living space.

My client wanted color, but she didn't know how to bring it in. It's understandable: An open-concept, high-ceilinged space like this is intimidating to decorate because of all the different surfaces and expanses of wall. I believe you can—and should!—do accent walls in a big, open space, but you need to maintain a tight color palette to hold it all together. Wanting something a little feminine and soft, we settled on a scheme of predom-inantly pink and green, which happens to be one of my favorite color combinations.

Our instinct was to give the space a contemporary bohemian look, but we didn't want to be too on the nose with a specific style, so I wove in an Art Deco undercurrent. You'll also note some strong 1970s vibes, courtesy of a shaggy rug and a Mario Bellini–style sofa—both of which were chosen because my client was pregnant and craving a cushy, cozy room to lounge in.

Even though this was one of my earliest client projects, it is still one of my most-liked and shared designs on Pinterest and Insta-gram. In fact, new clients often reference this space as inspiration when I work with them—the ultimate compliment a designer can receive!

Create a vignette with symmetry and color. On this console, a pair of prints, twin pink pots, and a funky vintage sculpture create an Instagrammable moment. I love small vintage accessories because it can be hard to find big ones that are in great condition.

opposite

Talk about a dramatic before and after: Trimmed out with a composite white granite, this home's fireplace looked so cold and cheap—serious copy-paste vibes. However, we didn't have the budget to replace it, so I hid it with vinyl wallpaper that has the look of rose quartz.

left

As a content creator, my client wished for a "wow" wall mural to function as both art and a backdrop for photos and videos. I sketched these graphics out beforehand, using pops of orangey-yellow and coral that tie back to the rug. With the bench and side table beneath, this formerly unused corner is now a fun focal point.

opposite

Attention aspiring maximalists: This room is a great example of how multiple accent walls can be used in a large, open-concept space. Painting or wallpapering walls in a contrasting color or pattern breaks up a large space. No piece is too overwhelming because each design moment is balanced against the others, and because the color scheme is cohesive.

opposite

This bar corner was so hideous it seemed like the only solution was to rip it all out, but that would have caused a cascade of pricey renovations. Instead, I found a way to work with it. The cabinets were updated with a fresh coat of paint and new hardware, while I covered the bar front with the same pink quartz wallpaper as the fireplace.

right

The mirrored shelving was a serious challenge to overcome, but when I got the idea to use colored adhesive glass film, new possibilities opened up. Creating the strong lines of color made the shelves into a cool design element, not some mistake we were trying to hide. It's one of my most dramatic DIYs to date!

Let's talk about contrast: Notice how the dark-green wallpaper wall offsets the fab vintage Italian dining chairs and creates visual depth. If you've got something you want to highlight, be sure to place it in front of a contrasting backdrop. The wallpaper's Art Deco–ish design had just a hint of pink that pulled the palette one stitch tighter.

opposite

If you're wondering what I mean when I talk about a "tight palette," take a look at these details: Every little thing is either pink or green. I'm always trying to marry a room's colors together—even in the tiniest accessories. Part of the key to successful maximalism is this purposeful restraint in even the smallest details.

right

Before I got my hands on it, this house had no decorative lighting: It was all recessed cans. Here I hung two Wink pendant lights at different heights, to bring your eye upward. While the Wink design is decidedly postmodern, the fringe felt like a nod to our Art Deco inspo, too.

A BOHO-DECO MASH-UP
TIPS & TRICKS

Explore the power of a pair

If you're stumped about a color palette, pick two colors and really commit to them like I did here. Once you've got that color pairing established everywhere, you can sprinkle in accent colors successfully.

Do decorate the floor

I've talked about the importance of the fifth wall in a room, aka the ceiling, but the floor is just as vital. Think of the floor as an open space for you to decorate and bring in color. In this space the showstopper rug was key to the whole design. I especially love rugs with abstract designs and bright colors.

Doll up your drywall

Limewash is tricky to apply because it is painted on with a brush for a purposefully textural effect, but it's worth the effort because it makes plain old walls almost look like plaster. If you're artsy, this is something you can DIY, but you can also hire a pro.

Make cabinets cute

You'll see lots of kitchen makeovers that feature painted cabinets, but I think people sometimes don't realize they can paint *any* built-in cabinetry—in *any* room. We had the cabinet doors in the bar area professionally spray painted for a completely fresh look. You can also do it yourself, but be sure to sand them well first and use a paint gun or sponge roller for a smooth finish.

Background refresh

We made over the back of the mirror bar shelves with adhesive glass film, but you can use this tactic with plain shelf backs and wallpaper or paint too. Simply add your accent to the back of any built-in shelves for a fun way to add contrasting color to a room.

Use lighting to define spaces

I used a bunch of tricks to create "rooms" within this open-concept space, but one room-defining feature you might not notice right away are the light fixtures: I used one big chandelier over the living area and centered another two fixtures over the dining nook, reinforcing the rooms within the room.

Art is the finishing touch in every room. I love to make my clients a custom piece that fits the vibe of their space perfectly, like this faces painting. It's an affordable way to add an extra layer of personalization.

A MAXIMALIST MANSION

When my client unexpectedly found himself with a house and the money to decorate it, I created a joyful home for his future.

This project has a wild backstory. My client discovered me watching *Trixie Motel*. He and his fiancé loved the exuberant rooms I designed for the show, but they never imagined they would be in a place to hire me.

Then quite unexpectedly, my client inherited several homes and a sizable amount of money. While the windfall was welcome, the larger story is more complicated. When my client's father passed away years ago, the majority of his estate went to my client's half brother. Two decades later, his half brother, whom he hadn't spoken to in years, died unexpectedly, and my client ended up inheriting it all as the next of kin—a total surprise.

This lake house was one of several properties my client inherited. It had fallen into disrepair, so renovation was a must. My client told me reviving the house in his hometown would feel therapeutic in a lot of ways. He wanted to make it a colorful, queer paradise

in this little Alabama town. As if this project couldn't get any more meaningful, my client's boyfriend proposed during the walk-through.

Decorating this house has been a journey for both of us. Architecture was my guide. In the part of the house with the grand vaulted ceilings, I was more traditional in my design. Whereas in the den, with its river rock fireplace and chestnut beams, I leaned into the midcentury era. The kitchen bridges the more old-fashioned rooms and the retro den. Elsewhere, I've indulged the couple's personal interests. All of it is just bursting with color.

It was a truly hands-on project with a dream client. I had so much fun picking all these special furnishings and just going wild because this client trusted me so much. I think this project gave him the house of his dreams, allowed him to make peace with the past, and set the stage for his future: He and his fiancé plan to get married here!

above/right

This is the first room you see when you walk in, so I wanted to make a maximalist statement, but in a really classy, sophisticated way. I built this living room around my scallop print, which appeared first as a tile in my Haustile collection and later as an upholstery fabric in my Joybird collaboration—both of which shine in this room. When I found this beautiful House of Hackney wallpaper that didn't fight too much with the scallop, I knew it was the perfect thing for the walls.

opposite

I wanted to keep some of the original elements that felt true to the house and its era, including the parquet floors. I also left the original fan because it was such a cool relic, with brass detailing and this carousel-esque rod holding it up.

The reading room was already blessed with cool original trim and built-ins, but they were super dark and dreary. So we painted them and added this Divine Savages wallpaper to the ceiling. I say don't feel guilty about painting a home's wood paneling, if it's not your style. Notice how the lampshades have the same pattern in a different color.

DAZEY DIY

Fake some fancy details. I bought six of the same mirror and had hung them at regular intervals, so they seem like this built-in special decorative moment.

opposite

The star of the dining room is the bespoke swan mural. It's partly inspired by the swans on the nearby lake and also an homage to the flamingo mural at the Trixie Motel. Then, me being me, I turned the mural into a repeat design and had it made into a custom wallpaper for the ceiling!

The kitchen is the one place where we made big structural changes. Originally a weird triangle shape with a big butler's pantry *and* a giant laundry room, we knocked down those walls and made it into an open-concept kitchen and den.

The kitchen is like a portal between the more traditional part of the house and the funkier retro area, so I wanted to strike a balance between the two: These wooden Reform cabinets were a mix of both of those worlds.

DAZEY DIY

Create a custom table. I had a piece of the countertop terrazzo cut into a circle to make the tabletop for the breakfast nook, lending the room a welcome consistency.

Our contractor built a custom banquette for this corner of the kitchen. We also created a built-in arched shelf for storage behind the bench. The cushions feature my signature stripe.

The Fireclay tile from
the kitchen backsplash
reappears in the
adjoining bathroom,
tying these two spaces
together. How cool
is this corner sink we
found that makes the
most of this small
space?

Now open to the kitchen, this den area is a casual place to chill out. I opted for a hardwood floor in this part of the house to replace the dirty old carpet. I chose herringbone because it felt like a good match to the parquet; we stained it to match the same tone. It also adds a subtle layer of pattern to the space.

I appreciated the river rock fireplace and the natural wood of the beams and window trim, so we kept them as they were. I designed the kitchen cabinets nearby to coordinate with the existing chestnut-hued wood.

The funky checkerboard wallpaper opposite the fireplace also appears in the kitchen (I love that it looks like it's painted!). On the ceiling is one of my own designs, but in a grasscloth paper for an extra boost of texture.

Notice how the green and blue sofas and pink ottomans coordinate with the rug and the wallpapers on their respective walls? This side of the space is the first of my experiments with whole-room color blocking—with patterns!—and I am so excited by the results. It's like each section of the room is its own stripe of color.

above

We took down the nonstructural walls in this part of the house to create a massive rec room.

opposite

The bar at the center encapsulates the unique palette. My client wanted a colorful room inspired by the pride flag, but not an overt red-orange-yellow-green-blue-purple rainbow.

This corner is all about gaming. My client wanted a big table for playing cards, so I found this amazing dining table and vintage dining chairs that perfectly coordinated with our color scheme. Tucked in one corner is a Dolly Parton pinball game and in another a gown once owned by Britney Spears, which I had designed a custom glass enclosure for.

DAZEY DIY

Make an extra-grand ceiling mural. After having the ceiling painted with a radiating starburst design, I further embellished it with a ceiling medallion and decorative trim pieces.

opposite

Using purple in the twin-bed bedroom was a little risky because it could have easily felt juvenile. For an elevated, adult feeling, I chose rich, deep elements like the rug and the beautiful ornate wallpaper.

This room is also a great example of the power of complementary colors: The many shades of yellow and purple just look so pretty together.

left/below

For the coordinating pattern-filled bathroom, I embraced purple's regal vibe with brass accents. Note that the vanity and toilet are very neutral here: You could enact a similar makeover without changing any plumbing.

For the primary suite, we started out with a more pink-dominated scheme, but we ended up going with deeper and cozier greens and blues as the main hues and pale pink as an accent. The bed canopy, heavy drapes, and House of Hackney wallpaper overhead reinforce the cocooning feeling of this room.

The adjoining primary bathroom has a slightly lighter color scheme with lots of flattering pale pink elements, including a gorgeous wallpaper that was designed for this room but is now a permanent part of my Spoonflower collection. It's nothing like the all-black windowless space this room was before—it was s-c-a-r-y!

Now, this is a fun room! We turned one of the guest bedrooms into a Dolly Parton–themed music room for my client, who is a lifelong and hardcore Dolly fan. The pink piano is the centerpiece for the room, but the hardest part might have been narrowing down which Dolly albums to frame and hang on the wall. (He had a huge collection!)

DAZEY DIY

Quadruple down on wall adornment. The lower half of the wall is painted pink, and I put light pink trim on top of it, creating a pattern-like effect. Then I paired this floral striped wallpaper with this butterfly one on the ceiling and a flower-power rug, for a total of four prominent prints.

This nearby bathroom is also lightly inspired by Dolly: I tied in the pink and then leaned into feminine, floral motifs.

We went with a flower theme with *everything* in this bathroom, from the toilet and sink right down to the trash can.

opposite/left

This room is all about the blue stripes, which I created in a variety of ways. We've got striped textiles (including the bed upholstery), painted stripes, and perhaps my favorite—the fluted wood trim, which we used both vertically and horizontally.

below

In the adjoining guest bathroom, we used more of the fluted wood trim. Here, the squiggle stripe wallpaper acts as a bridge between the stripes and the scalloped edge of the mirror.

The hallway is a moment where I really got to play with design. I pitched the idea of a color-changing hallway to my client and they loved it. I matched each part of the hallway to the room that's closest.

For example, the library room and the blue room have the blue hallway, giving you a taste of what the room color schemes are going to be as you're walking through.

I LOVE A PLAYFUL BATHROOM

My client's maximalist mansion had seven bathrooms that all needed to be gut renovated. I had SO much fun creating unique designs for each one. I believe that bathrooms have always been a place where people feel freer to express themselves. If you look at vintage bathrooms, they'll often have joyful colored tile and wacky wallpaper. Even the most serious restaurants will often have a statement bathroom.

Don't be afraid to customize each bathroom in your house and have fun with it. It's a bathroom, after all! Make it match the adjoining room—or don't! I enjoyed coordinating them here, but none of the baths necessarily match one another: They're all very different, and in some instances intentionally so.

Even if you don't plan to renovate, you can paint, wallpaper, hang a fabulous shower curtain, install glam lighting, swap out a boring mirror, invest in new hardware, or just add color through a bunch of small accessories and textiles. The lesson is: Don't settle for a boring bathing space.

Outside everything is done up in pink and two shades of green, from the exterior paint down to the waterline tile on the pool. The scallop and stripe patterns relate back to what's happening on the inside of the house.

As always, I treated the outside areas like extensions of the house, complete with outdoor rugs, cushions, and lighting to make it easy to entertain outdoors. Because this home will be a vacation home, we really doubled down on lounge and entertaining furniture.

A MAXIMALIST MANSION
TIPS & TRICKS

Embrace joy

My client's desire to create this proud queer paradise in the middle of Alabama really inspired me. You can (and should) use your decor to create the emotions you want to feel. Creating joy and celebrating who my client is was the driving force behind this whole home.

Work with two strong prints

The living room in his house features two of what I call "main character" prints, but the reason it works is that the scale is super different while the color schemes are the same. You can use two bold prints if you can vary the scale within a tight color theme.

Custom-order a rad rug

I've mentioned my love of Moroccan rugs before, but did you know you can custom order them through Etsy? I find makers who will take bespoke orders and then choose the yarns that are closest to my color scheme, like the pink and green rug in the formal living room.

Use your island

A lot of people don't realize that you can put a stove within an island, but you can, and sometimes it's the best place to have it, as was the case in this home.

One print, many colors

Throughout this house I used a single wallpaper print in a variety of different color-ways. This is a great way to dip your toes into my maximalist style of mixing patterns because the print and colors are already perfectly calibrated to each other.

Mix high and low

Of all my projects, this house is really the biggest high-low design with some very fancy pieces (hello, Murano glass chandeliers!) paired with some surprisingly affordable finds (the cute Target chairs in the library). Just because you have a bigger budget doesn't mean you have to splurge on everything.

HURLEY HOUSE

Designed for a pair of newlywed performing artists, this house is my maximalist take on rocker decor.

I've designed homes for performers of all kinds and plenty of music lovers, but this was my first time having a bona fide rock star for a client. When Andy Hurley, drummer for Fall Out Boy, and his wife, Meredith, a performing artist in her own right, contacted me about their home, I was excited to stretch my design in a little bit more of a rocker direction.

Meredith had rented My California Bungalow Gone Wild for a girls' weekend, and she emailed me while she was staying there to ask if I would consider working on their new home. Andy and Meredith were moving from a midcentury home in Portland that they'd never really gotten around to decorating. The new house, while luxurious and well laid out, was not really them: They're a very cool, eclectic couple, and they wanted their home to reflect that.

Working with some of their existing furnishings, I designed a home that was packed with personality on a tight timeline. I had particular fun playing with wallpaper in this space. Two themes that guided the design were the couple's love of animals (you'll see animals or animal print in every room) and that cool rocker edge that my clients both embody. It's hard to believe that this was just a white, sterile box just a few short months before they moved in.

As tends to happen with projects, the scope expanded. I started off designing the common area rooms, then they liked those so much we added on the primary suite, and now they want me to do the rest of the house.

This room is the first thing you see when you enter the home. To display Andy's collection of guitars, I framed the wall above the fireplace with trim and added a wallpaper panel, creating a strong focal point. The almost psychedelic wallpaper pattern on the lower wall lent the whole space that rock-and-roll vibe I wanted to achieve.

I designed for the room's super-high ceilings by adding the half wall trim, so the wallpaper didn't overwhelm the double-height space. Replacing the canned lighting with these pendants and a swooping chandelier helped visually bring down the high ceiling and added interest overhead.

opposite/left

Andy and Meredith wanted animal prints and motifs throughout the house, and I thought it would be fun to pair them with a tropical wallpaper in the dining room—literally putting the animal in a jungle. The rattan peacock chairs reinforce the tropics vibe.

above

A ceiling like this with a soffit around the perimeter is just begging for adornment. I played up the architecture with a two-tone paint job on the soffit and cheetah wallpaper inset in the center. A luxe ceiling medallion was the cherry on top.

The collection of neon signs that Andy and Meredith had made for their wedding was the spark for the den's design. I picked up the red hue from the lights and ran with it, using blush pink to mellow it out just a bit. The vintage Moroccan rug was a lucky find that brought the two dominant colors together.

This room plays with stripes in a bunch of different ways. I created a bold stripe on the ceiling using the existing beams and added bands of color to the backs of the built-in shelves with colored adhesive glass film. The curtains and throw pillows are also deliciously candy striped.

This breakfast nook is a testament to the power of paint plus textiles. We kept the existing banquette and table, but painting the walls a dusty pink and the banquette the same green as the cabinets instantly updated the all-white corner, while the striped tablecloth and bench cushions really bring out the personality. Giving the cushions and the table covering a wavy edge is that extra level of detail that makes it feel "wow."

The kitchen already had a great layout, cabinetry, and appliances—and this cool tile floor. My concept was to create a cabana-meets-country kitchen: Ruffles for a little country charm and cabana stripes for that Palm Springs vibe.

We had the cabinets professionally painted to alternate between pink and green, but what really ties the room together is the Mitchell Black wallpaper on the ceiling, which I had custom color-matched to the room. Bringing in the grays and the blacks from the counter and window frames makes it all feel super-intentional.

opposite

I designed this wallpaper for Andy and Meredith: They loved florals and stripes and I wanted to give them something that used both patterns and still felt uber-cool. I picked up colors from Andy's platinum albums and other awards and used them in the wallpaper.

right

My design for the lounge area off the primary bedroom evolved when Andy and Meredith told me they really wanted to use this room to play video games and cuddle with their dogs. I knew we should go full-on with the biggest couch we could fit. I used my favorite color blocking trick when ordering the sectional and pulled the colors up to the walls for a full-room striped effect.

When we settled on the primary bedroom's palette of green, pink, and orange, which relates to the adjacent lounge area, I had one of my wallpaper prints customized for this room. I decided to do just one section above the headboard to create a real focal point around the bed.

I didn't want to lose that rocker vibe in the bedroom, so I sprinkled in a classic checkerboard print that always feels a little rock and roll. Meredith asked for a cowprint chair, but it was tricky to find one that was chic, that wasn't actual cowhide, or that didn't have gold on it (a color they didn't like). I finally found this black and white one that ties back to the checkerboard beautifully.

In the primary bath, I ripped out the seriously sad gray tile floors and countertop, but I kept the vanity and tub to keep costs down. Removing the plain-Jane, wall-to-wall mirror and adding wallpaper transformed the walls. Then the black mirror, art, and light fixtures tied in the black window frames and gave the room a punch of contrast.

HURLEY HOUSE
TIPS & TRICKS

Befriend an upholsterer

For this project we ended up reupholstering some of my clients' existing furniture. While not always a cost-saver, custom upholstery is such a great way to give new life to things you love—and it results in pieces that are totally unique to your home.

Embrace what's there

All of the doors and windows in this house were black metal and we had no plans to change them, so I wove that into my design. Using even a tiny bit of black in each space helps make those architectural elements sing with the rest of the design.

Add some midtones

Another way I worked with the black was to use some muted and darker colors in some spaces, giving the design a little bit of weight and interest. Those darker hues also balance out the fluffiness of the playful pinks.

Fabrics come first

When developing a color palette, start with your fabrics, especially if you're crunched for time. There's a much more limited number of color options in fabrics. It's easier to find a paint color or to match your fabric than the other way around.

Create "frames" for wallpaper

If you don't want to do a full room or even an entire accent wall in wallpaper, you can "frame" a section of wallpaper with trim. In both the living room and the primary bedroom I used decorative trim to create distinct frames for wallpaper in places where it felt natural: above the fireplace and over the headboard.

Use the paint chip strip

I often use the same color throughout a house to make the design cohesive, but there are times when you might want a darker or lighter version of a color. I like to pick two colors from the same paint chip strip, rather than randomly pick two different shades. It's one small way that I bring consistency when there's so many different things going on.

THE DAZEY DREAM HOUSE

I've had so much fun designing my latest home, where my pattern designs appear in every single room.

I've included several of my personal homes (both past and present) in this book, but this one is our current home and perhaps my boldest yet.

When we moved, we wanted a place that would give us some flexibility, and this house with its separate living suite downstairs offered us a lot of options for wherever the future takes us. A 1920s house that has been added onto and remodeled over the years, it's got a little bit of a Craftsman style and a touch of that Los Angeles Spanish influence. I was especially drawn to the tall ceilings and subtle mountain vibe of the main room upstairs.

Renovating this house has been an exhilarating project because it is much more substantial than our previous home. This is a real House with a capital H: There's so much room to grow, explore, and play!

I wanted this house to be grown-up and even a little regal, but still my signature style. Certain elements of the house feel traditional, but I've injected them with freshness. With my first wallpaper and collection debut, I also wanted every single room in this house to have a pattern (or two!) of my own design. With my wallpaper on every wall and my personal artwork in many rooms, this home feels like a true expression of myself.

Figuring out what to keep, what to renovate now, and what to save for later has also been an interesting challenge. For example, the previous owner opened up the ceiling and added wood paneling and faux beams, which we loved. I didn't want to touch that! Past renovations and additions have made a hodgepodge of the flooring, so that is something we hope to redo at a future date. It's an evolving work in progress, and I can imagine us being here for a very, very long time.

DAZEY DIY

Make a plant threshold. I hung wall ledges over the opening to the dining room and filled them with plants. The vines trailing down create a cool transition between the spaces. You could do this over a doorway too!

The color palette shifts in a dynamic way from the main living area to the adjoining rooms. I used minty green, deep emerald, and dusty yellow in the main room, swapping yellow out for pink in the dining room and layering in a terracotta red (chosen in part to make my beloved Joybird chairs work in this space!). The nearby nook is all decked out in the same pinks and red, while the kitchen shifts back to the main room's scheme.

The dining room ceiling seemed like the perfect place for wallpaper. I matched the paint to my wallpaper design for a continuous field of color that gives this room an intimate ambiance—especially at night.

We sanded and refinished the original floors, but there was no way to fully hide their age and imperfections, so we got some huge carpets to cover them up and buy us some time. Plus, I was just so charmed by the wavy edge on this rug!

opposite

The double-height living room was what made us want to take a look at this listing in the first place. The beamed ceilings reminded me of my childhood home, and it felt really different from a lot of other spaces we were looking at. Adding skylights made the room even more enchanting.

Phillip and I added some elaborate wainscotting by painting different-sized stripes on the wall and adding little wood trim between each stripe. I also selected a low-profile sofa to reveal the half wall detail and to minimize the visual space taken up by the couch.

right

Meet my favorite nook. This pink velvet daybed fits this alcove like a glove. Now I take my work calls and have long, lazy conversations with friends here.

I wanted the kitchen to feel like an old Italian kitchen that your quirky grandma might have had. I based the yellow-green palette, which the kitchen shares with the living room, off the cement tiles.

The kitchen is always where everyone wants to hang out, so we opened up the wall to the dining room. To help it feel inviting and comfortable, I designed a built-in booth with a cute little tabletop and added some barstools at the new counter. Now there's room for everyone to gather.

Kitchen design is a little like playing *Tetris*: You have to puzzle out how to make it all fit just so. In this kitchen we paid extra attention to where the appliances went so that I could fit in all the things I have dreamed of having in a kitchen.

below

We loved the emerald green tile in the bathroom, so we kept it, but I updated the room with a new minty terrazzo floor and a vanity topped with the same material. Then we swapped the lighting and all the hardware for matching gold-hued ones that made this mini-makeover feel like a fully custom design.

opposite/above

I wanted our bedroom to feel f-a-n-c-y—fussy even!—so when I found a cool, spade-shaped decorative trim I snapped it up for the chair rail molding. The ceiling rosette is another pretty piece of decorative trim that makes the room.

At first, I designed curtains that were a different print for both this room and the living room, but when I hung them there were *too* many prints—I admitted defeat! I pivoted to designing a curtain that mimicked the stripes on our half wall. Now the wall stripe continues up and creates this lovely, thoughtful detail.

DAZEY DIY

Craft semicustom built-ins. Phillip built a frame along the wall to enclose two ready-made armoires into the walls. With wallpaper and paint it looks like a proper built-in, but it costs a fraction of full custom carpentry—even if you hire out the wall framing to a handyman. Replacing hardware and painting the doors made a major upgrade too.

opposite

I was excited to have a dedicated workspace in our new house, but old houses being what they are, we were also in need of some extra closet space. So, I came up with the idea of combining the two in this room. By building a wall of closets, I was able to achieve my dream of having an ultra-girl-y closet *and* a home office. Painted with color blocks, the closet doors just look like a cool backdrop to my desk, which makes a great folding table on laundry days.

left

The fancy frame pieces on the lower half of the walls are not original! They come as a finished piece that you just paint and attach to the wall.

above

I was able to sneak in this grand chandelier into a small room by centering it over the desk. With the wallpapered ceiling and the fluted medallion, it looks decadent, but if you touch it, you'd discover the crystals are actually acetate!

We suspect the previous owner, who was a musician, used this bonus space under the garage as a music room because there's a mini stage at one end and shelving underneath it that perfectly fits records. Phillip and I figured, *Why not lean into the retro theme?* I pulled the pattern from my sofa onto the walls and curtains for a monoprint effect.

Part of the beauty of a modular couch is that it can adapt easily to a new space. We put four sections of my Joybird sofa on the lower level and tucked two on top. It feels custom made to the space, but it's just the modular pieces doing their thing.

This room had weird, dark faux-wood floors that did not match the house at all. I considered shag carpet to hide it, but when I saw these funky striped carpet tiles from FLOR they were such a perfect match for my pattern. Plus, I love that we can swap out a tile if we spill something on it.

For this guest bedroom, I designed the wallpaper with this infinity-retro vibe to it and had my wavy checkered print color-matched to it as a secondary print for the bedding. I'd originally planned to paint the floors but when I saw these groovy FLOR carpet tiles designed by Trina Turk in a similar color, I decided to do carpet instead.

Sometimes more *isn't* more: When I added that checkered rug, it actually made all the crazy patterns clashing seem layered and intentional and less busy.

I wanted to add color to the bedroom ceiling, but I didn't want it to get too dark, so I went with a high-gloss emulsion. The light reflects off it so that it's not too dark or as intense as a lighter red color would have been.

below

I visually divided the main living area by shifting to this cool, graphic stripe wallpaper for the dining area and a desk nook, then I added the stripe as curtains in the more granny area to tie them together. Rugs and unique light fixtures over the sitting and dining areas further define the spaces.

above

The lower level had very industrial, basement-y vibes before; our goal was to make it really cozy and warm. However, I wanted to use some cool-toned blues because I planned to hang my grandmother's blue paintings here. My solution was to develop a quirky take on an Americana palette of red, white, and blue with pops of warm mustard yellow.

To bring this crazy color scheme together, I designed a custom wallpaper with a very granny look. Then I was very strategic with the pillows, art, and all the other accents I used in this room.

opposite

This was just an ugly gravel driveway before we decided to make it an additional outdoor living space. After removing and leveling the old gravel, we laid a checkerboard of ready-made concrete pavers and then cut pieces of faux turf to fill in the other squares. Repeating stripes on the cowboy pool, and pillows, create a resort-like feeling with a playful high-low vibe.

right

Our house was originally gray stucco with bright, angry red trim, and the way that it was built into the hillside, it stuck out in a bad way. We painted it light green with a darker green for the trim and deck to tone it down and have it blend in more to the trees.

left

Look closely: That's not tile on the covered deck floor. Phillip and I painted that design right onto the concrete with a stencil to get the look of tile more affordably.

THE DAZEY DREAM HOUSE
TIPS & TRICKS

The old one-two punch

When mixing prints, I always like to think of a primary and secondary print. The primary is the main character print, which is more complex and illustrative. The secondary is the companion print—something less bold and usually a different scale.

Get some plants already!

A houseplant adds color and makes a space feel more homey without making any drastic changes to any of the walls. Plants breathe literal life into a space and help it feel complete. If your rooms don't have any greenery in them, get yourself to your local plant shop—stat!

Make your home a gallery

This house is bursting with my personal design—and it feels so good. People are often hesitant to display their own artwork, but I say use the walls of your home to broadcast your creativity.

Stripes cut sweetness

I designed some almost-old-fashioned floral wallpapers for this house, but they're often purposefully paired with a stripe. A strong, graphic pattern, like a stripe or a check, has the power to temper the sweetness of a floral-y print.

Double the fun

Half walls abound in this home because I wanted to max out my opportunities for pattern and color play. Adding a half wall to a room in your home is a great way to start experimenting with design on a more complex level.

Appreciate the bedroom set

Matching bedroom sets have a very 1980s reputation (and not in a good way!), but if the furniture is cool, a coordinate set can be a smart strategy to help a maximalist bedroom feel more uniform.

Reconsider wall-to-wall

I am predicting a carpet comeback. People love rugs, so why not consider a completely carpeted room? Everything in design circles back around, and I think wall-to-wall is due to be done in a new way.

2/

STAY

MY DAZEY DESERT HOUSE

This midcentury house launched my interior design career. It's also the home with the kitchen renovation that made everyone mad.

My Dazey Desert House was the first home I ever owned and my first major residential design project—talk about a special place! I hadn't aspired to buying a house in Palm Springs, but after years of trying (and failing) to purchase a home in Los Angeles, a trip to the area during Modernism Week inspired the inevitable Zillow search. I'd spent a ton of time in Palm Springs because my mom grew up there. So, when I spotted this classic midcentury house designed by William Krisel, a noted architect, I was intrigued. Here was a chance to own a piece of art by one of the greats. I hadn't planned to buy a vacation home before a primary home, but I am so glad (and fortunate) I was able to.

The house had great bones and an amazing location, but it was all white walls, gray floors, and zero personality, aside from its sunny orange front door (the one thing I haven't changed!). Over the last seven years, my husband, Phillip, and I have slowly renovated it, one project at a time, as our budget allows.

My goal has been to create a home that pays homage to the midcentury era, but in a fresh, contemporary way—it's a house, not a museum. I've loved playing with wallpaper, retro-inspired furnishings, new lighting, and fun floor tile. The results reflect what is now my signature style: A home that is bursting with color, personality, and joy. While I believe a house is never finished, I am so proud of what I've accomplished. We decided to share this house with others by renting it out as a vacation home when we're not there.

I wanted this home to feel like a visual feast from the moment you step inside. Drawing inspiration from the original front door, I leaned into orange with the decor. The tile floors are one of the first things visitors notice when they arrive (and one of the last things we added). I chose the oblong checkerboard because I wanted something that felt of the house's era yet also timeless. I had no idea what a hassle it would be to install (sorry, Phillip!), but it was worth it!

left

We kept the original kitchen as long as we could, but when the built-in oven died, it necessitated a full renovation. (Purists, please forgive me; I loved that William Krisel cook space, but I actually needed to, well, cook.) People are often afraid to commit to color in the kitchen, but I believe in making the home's most-used room a place that sparks joy.

opposite

Midcentury-esque Reform cabinets with multicolor doors create a kicky color block effect, while a few natural wood panels temper the candy colors. Add in the retro-looking Smeg appliances and the finished kitchen feels so 1970s that people often think this is the original.

This gallery wall is so special to me because all of the artwork is by my grandmother. My grandma has been a huge inspiration to me as an artist and designer: She was someone who loved color and knew how to use it. I think of this wall as a collaboration between the two of us. This vignette was one of the first things I did as an interior decorator but it's still one of my favorite walls.

HOW TO CREATE A GALLERY WALL

You'll notice that gallery walls appear in many of my projects and in all of my personal homes. I love hanging art in this style because it lets you put a lot of artwork onto one wall. Here are my tips for creating your own salon-style gallery.

START WITH A FUN BACKDROP

Actual galleries often feature plain white walls, but I like to arrange art on top of wallpaper or a brightly painted surface. I think it helps make the art pop.

AIM FOR A VARIETY OF SIZES

A salon-style hanging looks best if you have a nice mix of small, medium, and large artworks. I like to have at least one large-ish piece to anchor most of my gallery walls.

YOU DON'T NEED TO MEASURE

I try to keep the distance between frames relatively uniform (a couple of inches of breathing room), but I don't precisely measure anything. Instead, I lay it out on the floor to get the arrangement correct and snap a photo to re-create it on the wall.

CREATE SOME CONTINUITY

The beauty of a gallery wall lies in the eclectic mix of art and objects, but you can't just have a totally random wall of stuff. Try to find artworks with some shared colors, paint a few frames to match one another, and even include some pairs or trios within the larger arrangement.

FILL THE WALL

One thing that can go wrong with a gallery wall is if you don't have enough art. A little cluster of art on a big wall is always going to look skimpy. I think gallery walls look best when they take up most of the wall.

ADD SOME OBJECTS

Weaving in some non-framed art, like a textile, weaving, or other tactile object, adds major visual interest to a gallery wall.

KEEP ADDING

Another cool thing about a gallery wall is that it can evolve and grow over time. If you get a new photo or painting you love, you can rearrange to add it in.

A recent addition is the wall mural, which I painted myself. My trick is to draw it out first, then project the sketch onto the wall. If you don't own a projector, check with your local library, they sometimes have ones you can check out.

left

We use the third bedroom, which adjoins the primary bedroom, as both an office and guest quarters. I'd planned to close the opening between the two rooms, but after spending time here, my husband and I decided we liked having a grand primary suite. When we have a full house, we pull out the sofa bed and close the curtain between the two rooms—flexible space for the win!

opposite

In a little departure from the rest of the house, I brought cool tones into the primary bedroom. With a blue velvet headboard and teal wallpaper by Justina Blakeney, there's a magical feeling in this room. However, it still connects to the main living space thanks to its yellow and orange accents and the floor tile, which is the same design we used on the kitchen backsplash.

DAZEY DIY

Create a maximalist "headboard." An uninterrupted wall behind a bed with no windows or doors like this one is such a great spot for a single, wallpapered wall. It makes the whole wall feel like it's part of the headboard.

opposite

Our guest bedroom has a little bit of a Joshua Tree vibe, with its earthy-sunny palette and an all-around peaceful, happy vibe. I love that there's a different experience as you go into the bedroom—a little surprise for our guests.

right

The bathroom renovation was mostly cosmetic, including swapping out the old light fixtures and the sink. One of the coolest things we did was reglaze the sunken tub, an original feature we wanted to keep, in this fun shade of orange. Hello, sunshine!

opposite

A "cowboy pool" is a super-affordable way to add a pool to your backyard. We had a stock tank painted to match the front door, and my husband built a deck around it, two tricks that make a DIY stock tank pool feel so much more elevated.

left

Aside from the circular concrete pad beneath, this hot tub setting was created entirely from readymade elements. I add Softub Spa hot tubs to every project I can because they're so easy to install—it was a bonus that this one was available in orange. I also love that they kind of look like a big piece of upholstered furniture!

above

I wanted the backyard to be another living space to hang out in, so we created a series of room vignettes, including this funky fire pit from Boxhill surrounded by classic Acapulco chairs, both chosen in the house's signature tangerine.

MY DAZEY DESERT HOUSE
TIPS & TRICKS

Pick a color leader

From the moment I saw this house, I knew I was going to lean into the bright orange on the front door. Choosing a dominant color early on is an easy way to create cohesion in your home's design—and it gives you something to scout for when shopping, so you don't feel so overwhelmed by all of the choices!

Food for thought

I've always felt that color nourished me, and the book *Joyful,* by Ingrid Fetell Lee, confirmed this feeling when it revealed that humans have an especially good sense of color, which helped our ancestors find fruit and nutritious plants. "Color is an indication of the richness of our surroundings," writes Lee. "It is an unconscious signal not only of immediate sustenance, but an environment that is capable of sustaining us over time." Y'all, color literally feeds us.

Don't knock white walls

I love color, and this house is colorful to the max. However, you'll notice we kept a lot of the walls white. White walls felt right for the classic post and beam architecture, and I love how much light the white reflects into the space. Plus, with some major statement floors and accent walls, this space didn't need color on every surface.

Do over your doors

We kept the house's original doors but painted them all orange to match the front door. Painting doors a confident color is an easy and affordable way to give basic hollow-core doors personality.

Make an indoor-outdoor connection

One of my favorite things about California design is the indoor-outdoor lifestyle. To make the outside feel like an extension of the living space, I used the same colors and midcentury-inspired silhouettes in both places. Likewise, a few potted cacti indoors mimic the cactus garden outside.

Sprinkle in some hand-drawn elements

If a room feels a little stiff, add a hand-drawn element. As an artist, I'm a huge fan of hand-drawn design elements: They're whimsical while still feeling elevated and artistic. The desert illustration of the bedroom wallpaper adds welcome softness and organic shapes to the linear elements in this home.

Don't rush

On Instagram, makeovers happen in an instant, but IRL, things take more time—often *a lot* more time. The photos you see here show the Dazey Desert house as it is today, but there were so many iterations in between. Remember that when you start your own project.

While it looks retro, this couch is from a collection I created with Joybird. I love the style of vintage couches, but they can often be worn down, so I shop for vintage-*looking* upholstered pieces instead. (I tend to go genuine vintage for art and non-upholstered furnishings.) The white walls in this corner offer a moment of relief in the super-saturated living space, but I'll confess a part of me is tempted to add a supergraphic mural here one day.

THE TRIXIE MOTEL

This dream project pushed my design skills to the max and introduced my interior style to a much wider audience.

Getting cast as the designer on the television show *Trixie Motel* was a pinch-me moment. I'd always dreamed of doing a hospitality project, and the chance to do it as part of a renovation show in my beloved Palm Springs, with an amazing cast of characters, was just beyond.

Drag performer and singer Trixie Mattel and I share a similar aesthetic that is super retro-inspired, filled with saturated color, and very California girl. It was so rewarding to collaborate with someone who appreciates color and good design, and has an eye for quirkiness, done in a really tasteful, cool way.

The assignment really stretched me in new ways, and I even designed a custom pattern and a wall mural for each room! In the show, each room was its own episode, but we'd done months of planning leading up to the filming. The magic of television condensed and streamlined this project to make good TV, but the tight deadlines and budget were absolutely real.

The project opened so many doors: It led directly to me designing my first collection of home textiles and wallcoverings for Spoonflower and introduced me to some of my favorite clients. The Trixie Motel also ended up being super special to me because Phillip and I ended up getting married there on the TV show!

Here's how my biggest project came together and all the design lessons I learned along the way.

PINK FLAMINGO

opposite

This was the first space that we tackled at the Trixie Motel, and it established many of the key elements of the themed rooms: A wall mural, coordinating wallpaper and textiles (in a print designed by me, of course), and a custom stained-glass panel for the glass brick. There are broad strokes for now, but trust that I will get into All. The. Details. in the pages ahead.

right

The flamingo mural was such a key early piece of the Trixie Motel design. It inspired me to make a custom print for this room's bedding, curtains, and wallpaper, which in turn led to custom pattern designs for *every* room. We also quickly realized the rest of the murals should be much less complicated—this one took for-*ever* to paint. Learn from my mistake: Murals should be relatively simple!

If anyone other than a drag queen had purchased this motel, they probably would have added the dressing rooms onto the main part of the rooms, but Trixie loved the idea of a dedicated primping corner where guests could get fully done up, so we kept them but gave them a makeover.

I had the custom vanities made out of Formica, a type of laminate that was a popular countertop material in midcentury. Formica had fallen out of vogue, but it turned out to be the ideal material to create the funky shapes and the fun colors we wanted. I also loved that it nodded to the hotel's original era. You'll see these in every room.

A WORD ABOUT THEMES

I love a theme. I love to dress up for a themed party. I adore a holiday theme. Theme restaurant? Count me in. A theme is always fun. Trixie and Trixie's husband, David, had picked the themes for the Trixie Motel before I started working on the project, and it was cool and challenging for me to figure out how to make these different themed rooms feel well thought out and elevated. They wanted it to be very upscale—not pure kitsch.

I've often used specific eras or styles as a strong theme for a room, but when I do, I try not to go too far. I like to throw in some elements that aren't on theme, things that round it out a little so it doesn't feel too on the nose. I also pay extra attention to the quality of materials and finishing touches to make sure a themed room feels polished. If you do it carefully, you can pull it off in a way that doesn't feel tacky.

For inspiration for the Trixie Motel, I researched vintage hotel rooms of the era, and so many of them had matching bedspreads and wallpapers. As a print designer, I just loved that single-pattern look, so I pitched the idea of monoprint rooms to Trixie and David, and they loved it. We had the wallpaper, curtains, and bedding custom made.

above

I'll paint the big picture on these kitchenettes, and then we'll get into the finer details in the following pages. All of the suites had a kitchenette that was long overdue for a renovation: By eliminating the big, old appliances, I was able to carve out space for a little breakfast nook by the door that leads out to the patio. For consistency I used terrazzo countertops and patterned porcelain tile in all the kitchenettes.

right

There was a big debate over whether to keep the bathroom's original tile or rip it out and start fresh. The square tile was so perfectly vintage and in good shape, but they were showing their age and not quite the right shade of pink. We were on a pretty limited budget, so we decided to reglaze the original tile. I had never done reglazing before, and I was blown away by the process of being able to pick the exactly perfect shades we wanted for the bathrooms. Just look at the pink and mint combo!

QUEEN OF HEARTS

Our contractor had suggested drywalling over the brick, but I thought the texture was cool and it felt authentic to the midcentury era. I always keep as many of the original features as I can, but I update them for the modern day. People are hesitant to paint over brick, but at the Trixie Motel the brick was already painted, so I felt free to layer on the color.

above

The ceiling mirror and painted supergraphic were definitely cheeky additions to this room. I love to do a mural like this that goes over the architecture in unexpected ways. We got some help with this mural from my friends at Very Gay Paint.

right

Creating custom beds for the hotel was definitely a splurge, but they really made the rooms. Even if you're not going custom, I highly recommend a velvet headboard: You can find such rich, fun colors in velvet—not just boring beige and gray.

As a designer, I looked at the Trixie Motel almost like a branding project. That may not seem relevant to a home, but if you pick a motif and really run with it, it can make an interior feel more special. Likewise, instead of settling for generic art, commission something custom or semicustom, like these pieces depicting Trixie by illustrator Choriza May, a fellow drag queen, that adorn every room.

The best wall for a mural is the first one you see when you come into the room.

The Queen of Hearts room got the boldest reglazing: hot pink! I always say you can make any challenging part of a room work, and these irregularly shaped showers prove it with their daring new look, courtesy of reglazed colors, fresh fittings, and glass doors.

Replacing the old sinks with terrazzo countertops and vessel sinks cleared out space underneath the sinks, which helped make the small bathrooms feel a little more spacious. Plus, I personally love a vessel sink: I find them to be less splashy and messy than regular sinks.

WHEN THINGS GO WRONG

Anyone who watched *Trixie Motel* will remember the faux-razzo floor disaster, which I'd like to mention because decorating projects can and will go wrong from time to time. Trixie had wanted fun flooring, but tile and terrazzo were not in the budget nor possible in our tight timeline, so I came up with the idea of doing a fake terrazzo look with epoxy, like the kind used in garages with flecks in the paint and a super high-gloss finish. It's a commercial-grade flooring, but we ran into trouble getting the custom colors done. This was a time where I learned the hard way: The first attempt was a disaster of bubbling paint. Luckily, Trixie and David were down to give it another shot, and in the end we found the right mix of paint, but it was scary. Trixie took a chance working with me, so I needed to make it right. We ended up pivoting to use linoleum tiles in a bunch of the rooms, which turned out beautifully too. What I learned through this setback was that when things aren't going as planned, you just have to put on a brave face and push through.

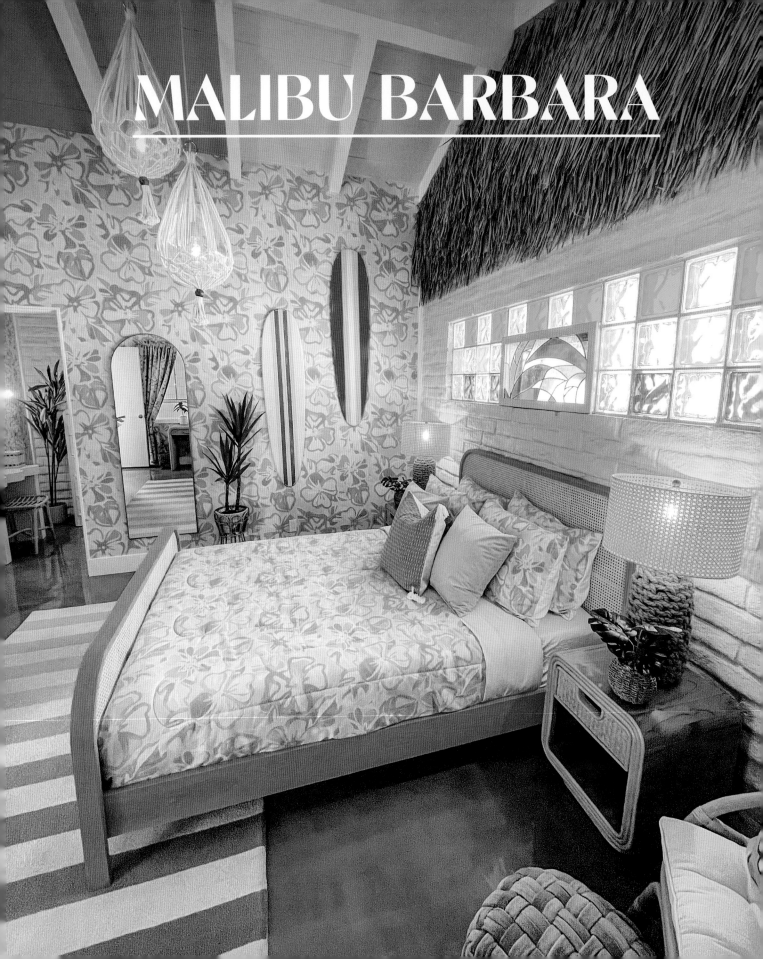
MALIBU BARBARA

The color scheme for this room was inspired by the packaging of a Malibu Barbie—punchy pastels with a distinctly '80s vibe. But I also made sure to weave in some natural elements like the caning panels on the bed frame and console table to make sure it still felt adult.

This room ended up having so many fun DIY decorating ideas to steal, like these decorative surfboards that I sourced from Etsy (way cheaper than buying real surfboards). The beachy grass effect under the eaves is thatch that I ordered online and nail-gunned directly to the wood.

above left

The post and beam ceiling looked extra fun painted in the Malibu Barbie palette. Leaving the beams white helped give the design structure and definition. I loved the macramé pendants because they looked like antique glass fishing floats.

above right

The giant palm tree and sunset wall mural in this room created a "view" from the bed. You can also create a view with a huge photo or painting of a landscape or a nature-themed wallpaper accent wall.

right

How cool is the striped effect we created in the bathroom by continuing the painted wall stripes onto the glass block? This is a design trick that I love: Anytime you can continue a painted element onto a new material or plane, it creates this very intentional and playful look.

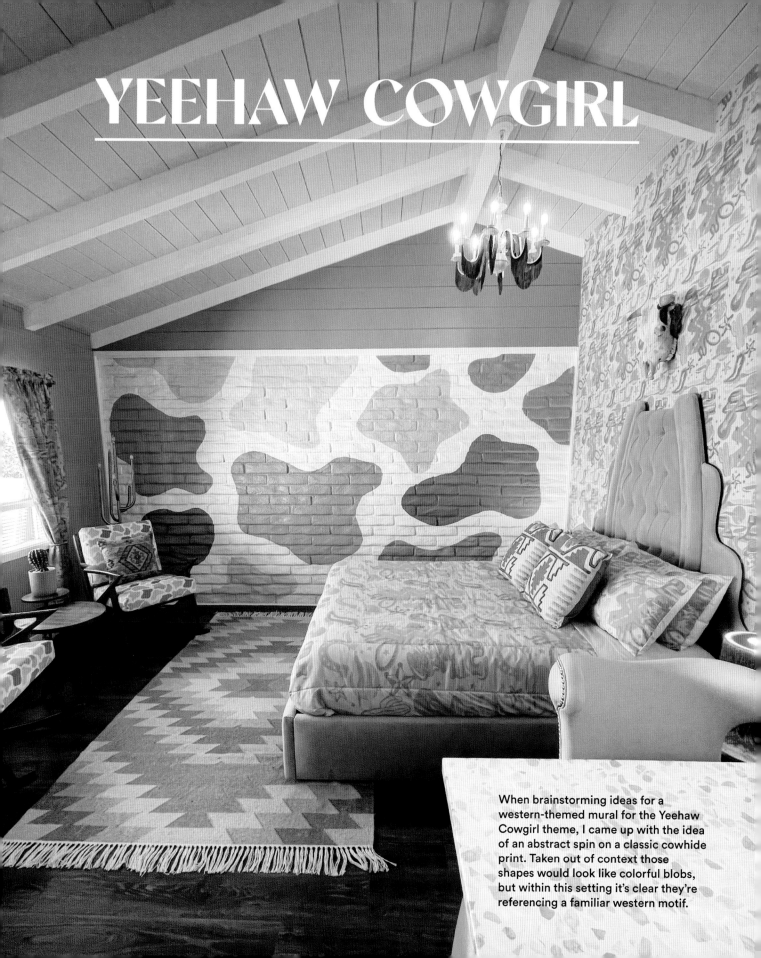

YEEHAW COWGIRL

When brainstorming ideas for a western-themed mural for the Yeehaw Cowgirl theme, I came up with the idea of an abstract spin on a classic cowhide print. Taken out of context those shapes would look like colorful blobs, but within this setting it's clear they're referencing a familiar western motif.

below

This bathroom really shows off the stained-glass panels we commissioned from Mojo Glassworks. I did this because the glass brick had these really ugly windows in the middle that we couldn't get rid of, so we had to work around them. The custom stained-glass pieces made what is kind of a dated look amazing. They're like a custom piece of artwork for every room!

right

A couple more earthy elements, like the skull and woven pillows, help bring the cotton-candy palette down to earth in the Yeehaw Cowgirl room.

This was one of the more resourceful DIYs we did at the Trixie Motel: We salvaged the tufted pleather bar front by painting it with a leather paint that Trixie had used on costume pieces before. It worked shockingly well! I found bar stools with a similar design to match the bar.

ATOMIC BOMBSHELL

opposite

These dupes of the iconic Eero Aarnio Ball Chair and the sputnik-style floor lamp instantly gave the Atomic Bombshell room that distinctive Atomic Era vibe we were going for.

right

A round bed is not something I'd necessarily recommend for everyday living (it's tricky to make them up!), but it was such a fun addition to this room. I designed the supergraphic behind the headboard to match the dimensions of the bed, a favorite trick of mine.

above left

The dressing room's warm metallic touches—starburst wall art, spray-painted faux cactus, and sconces—give the space a little extra glam. The dresser was a splurge from Jonathan Adler that I couldn't resist!

above right

In the Atomic Bombshell bathroom, I used a simple stripe on the brick to add extra visual interest; notice how I continued the stripe into the sink niche for continuity.

FLOWER POWER

The Flower Power suite shows off how we used linoleum tiles to great effect. Linoleum is not exactly seen as the pinnacle of design after a history of being used in places like schools and the DMV. However, linoleum is a durable, high-quality, and affordable material that comes in oodles of cool colors. I realized we could lay out the tiles in fun ways and use a bright palette to make them modern. Here, we made a super-sized checkerboard by putting four tiles of each color together to make bigger squares.

left

I designed all the suites with entertaining and the Palm Springs lifestyle in mind. Whenever I had space, I put a couple of chairs at the bar, so guests could enjoy a drink and socialize. Don't these vintage rattan chairs look so cute with a fresh coat of paint and new fabric on the seats?

opposite

I thought I was going to have this room on lock because so many of my print designs have floral patterns and my design aesthetic is very flower forward, but it ended up being one of the hardest to get right! We went through multiple color palettes and print designs. The oversized and more structured print that we finally chose makes this retro print feel a little more upscale.

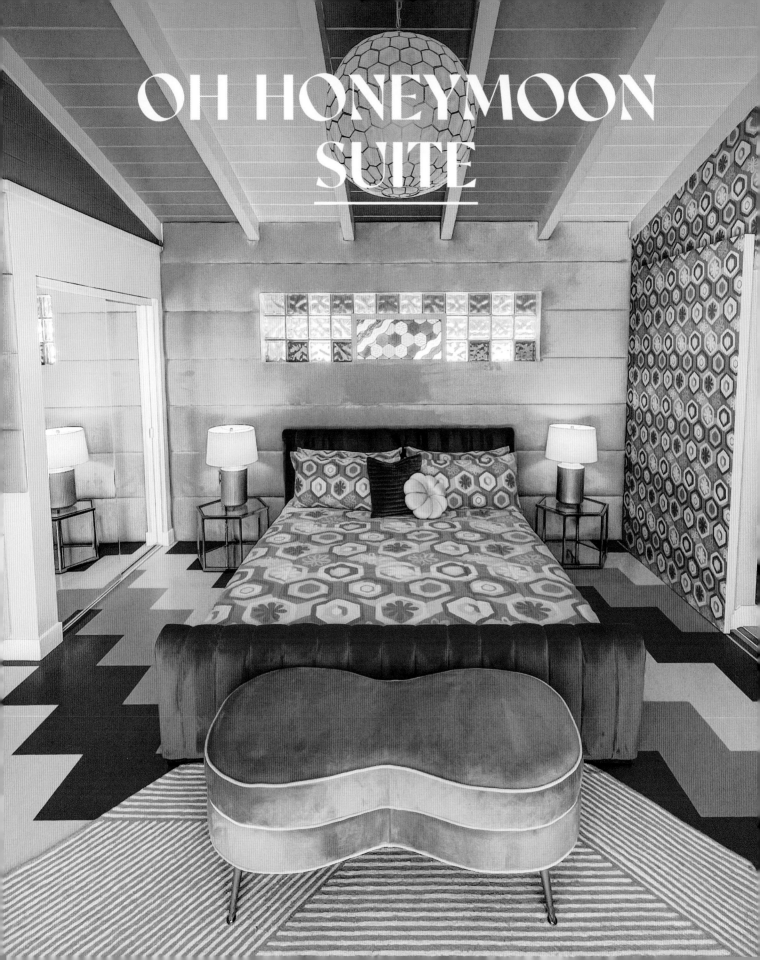

OH HONEYMOON SUITE

The Oh Honeymoon Suite had a more abstract theme than the others. In addition to the strong yellow in the color scheme, I played off bees and honeycombs in the custom print and accents for this room.

I never want to be too precise with a theme, so the "honeymoon" theme played out as a lot of hexagon motifs, including the pattern I designed for the wallpaper and textiles, the bathroom tiles, the mirror above the dresser, and even the glass on the overhead light fixture.

This room originally had two large closets, so I decided to demo one to make room for a little lounge area. The new cozy booth with a café table can be used for breakfast or to work on a laptop.

We really had fun with the linoleum tiles in this suite: We considered a three-colored checker and a chevron, but we ended up going with this zigzag pattern. What's so cool about these floor tiles is that you can lay them out in a ton of different ways.

This is the only room at the hotel in which we painted the beams a color. I wanted everything to be super warm and enveloping in this space, so I went with this soft butter-yellow instead of pure white, which would have contrasted too harshly.

This was the first bathroom I designed for accessibility, and I enjoyed the challenge of finding things like grab bars and a wheelchair-accessible sink that worked with my aesthetic.

Because we needed to move things around, this bathroom got new, three-color hex tiles that turned out so sweet: I love how they just create this warm field of undulating color. You could create the same effect with a cool scheme or even shades of white and cream, if you're not so bold.

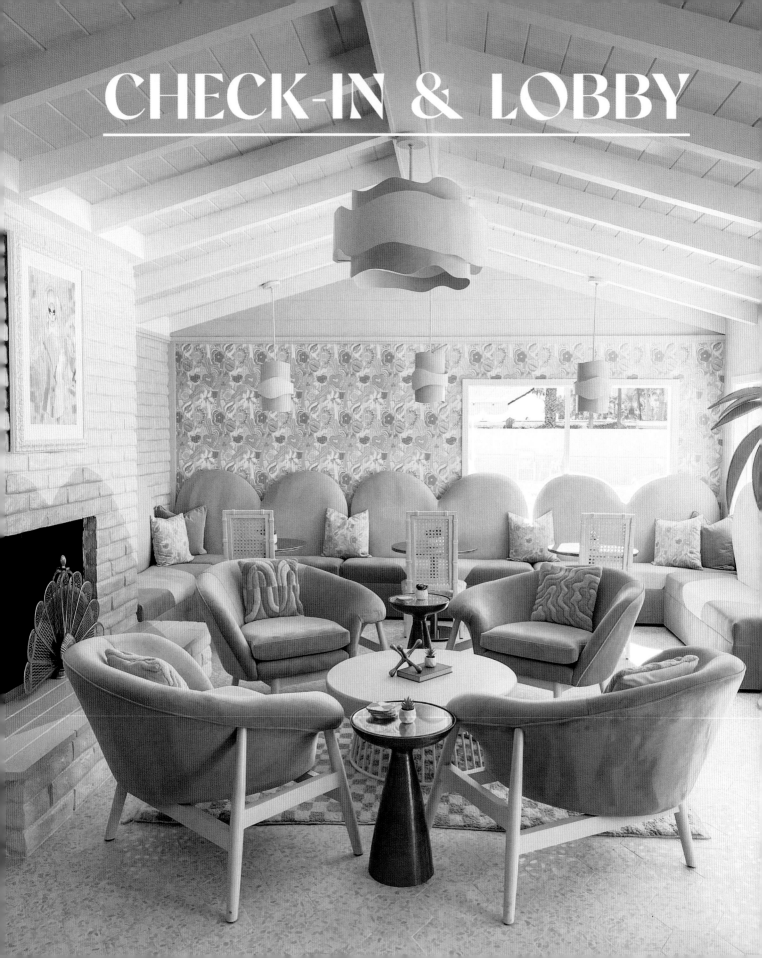

CHECK-IN & LOBBY

left

Our project manager, David Rios, found this gorgeous slab of mauve stone that we turned into the check-in desk. I designed the pattern you see on the floor as a signature print for the hotel. We had custom Trixie tiles made in a diamond shape that adds a little more interest than the standard square.

below

Trixie's extensive Barbie collection is her prized possession, but the dolls were just sitting in her closet. Trixie wanted to display them at the hotel. I came up with the idea to display the Barbies in little bell jars above the check-in area, so they would feel properly and lovingly displayed.

opposite

Trixie and David wanted to use this room: As a breakfast room for guests, a place to lounge during the day, a restaurant-bar at night, *and* potentially a performance space for drag shows. So, I settled on a grouping of four luxurious statement chairs in front of the fireplace with booths built in around the perimeter of the room to accommodate a lot of people in a relatively modest space.

The lobby lounge was originally this big brown and red room with a dingy leopard-print carpet. To lighten it up, I went with a monochrome blush scheme. A solid color field is a great choice for a public-facing room because it feels so transportive.

above

I designed the custom booths to look like jumbo-sized hearts: The top half of each heart was created with the cushion back shape and the bottom with a triangular panel in the upholstery. I worked with LA's Total Design Furniture on all of the custom pieces: Those guys can bring anything to life! The palm tree floor lamp was a vintage find that we painted to match the rest of the decor.

right

The caned chairs were a local thrift store find that I painted pink and had the seats reupholstered in the same print that we used on the walls.

The lobby and the custom wallpaper I designed for it pick up themes and motifs from various guest rooms—hearts, palm trees, and flowers—but the big lips supergraphic on the fireplace is all its own. One fun detail not to miss: We wallpapered the vintage arcade game to the left of the fireplace to match the room!

I loved the pool's super-retro kidney-bean shape, but the old girl was in need of a refresh. I added stripes of pink and white glass tile around the perimeter, pink penny tile on the steps, and heart tile on the bottom of the pool—and when I couldn't find any cool depth-marking tiles, I found Haustile, a company that could make custom porcelain tiles for us! The patio surrounding the pool was updated with fresh concrete. The resulting space is almost like a movie set. Sometimes Palm Springs doesn't even look like a real place—and especially so here, in this queer fantasy of a motel pool.

Aside from the concrete work, the pool area refresh is not all that different from a room makeover: We used a whole lot of pink paint and fun furnishings to make this outdoor space feel like the rest of the hotel.

THE TRIXIE MOTEL
TIPS & TRICKS

Materials matter

A themed design is more likely to feel tacky if you're using cheap materials. Since we wanted these rooms to be elevated, it was mission-critical to choose the highest-quality pieces and materials.

Revisit retro sources

We played with a lot of old-school materials at the Trixie Motel, including Formica and linoleum. Researching your home's original era can help you discover unique materials that will give it a place-appropriate vibe.

Curate your collections

When you want to incorporate a personal collection into your decor, you need to act like a museum curator. We didn't display every last one of Trixie's Barbies in the check-in area; rather, we picked the best ones and presented them in a way that highlighted the collection.

Seek out small vendors

We collaborated with a ton of small businesses for custom elements of the hotel, such as the Mojo Glassworks stained glass and the Haustile porcelain tiles. I find that indie businesses are so much more hands-on and take the time to make the pieces special. Plus, I love supporting amazing small businesses that are trying to make the world a more beautiful place!

Necessity is the mother of invention

The tight budget and timeline of a home renovation show led to some truly creative solutions I may not have thought up otherwise. Instead of lamenting a small budget or lack of time, think of them as creative challenges.

Grout is not just an afterthought

In the lobby, we laid the tiles with super thin grout lines, so that the pattern could really shine. There's nothing like a big, thick grout line to ruin a really solid repeat!

3/

WORK

WORK, PLAY, SLEEP, REPEAT

Real estate is real expensive these days. When my clever clients hatched a plot to create a hybrid space for their podcast, I helped to make their dream a reality.

Today, the lines between work and play are more blurred than ever. So it should come as no surprise that some enterprising millennials came to me with a live-work project. I met these clients, the co-hosts of a popular podcast, when they rented out my downtown co-working space, and we had stayed in touch over the years. They were making the move to a new office space for their podcast and they asked me to design the interiors. But this wasn't just going to be a workplace: One of the co-hosts would also be living there, so the space had to walk the line between personal and professional.

Located in a new building in Culver City, this was a cool setup where there were businesses on the ground floor and live-work lofts above. For this two-bedroom, two-bath space, they planned to use the primary suite as the host's personal quarters. I was tasked with decorating the public-facing rooms: An open-concept living, dining, and kitchen space; the second bedroom, which would be used as the podcast recording studio; and a guest bathroom.

These ladies have super-sophisticated tastes and wouldn't normally decorate quite so colorfully in their homes, but they desired a playful space for their podcast. These women knew that having bright, interesting spaces to create content in would help their brand stand out and make it easy for their podcast guests to snap cute selfies. My challenge was to bring in color and life but keep it refined and grown-up at the same time. I think we succeeded!

left

For these clients, I wanted to design cute backdrops that still felt mature, like this simple squiggle graphic. Once it was painted on the wall, I placed shelves within the wall graphic. Styled with plants and accessories, it creates this cool visual feast with a 3-D mural effect. It's one of my designs that I've seen re-created most often!

opposite

The dining table does triple duty as a conference table, a place to eat, and a buffet for events, so it was an extra-important part of the design. I found an amazing vintage, marble-top table with executive-but-elevated vibes on Facebook Marketplace. However, it wasn't quite right, so I ended up buying a fluted brass base and putting the marble top on that instead. The original table base is now the console. Remember this when shopping secondhand: You don't have to use a piece exactly as it was designed.

below

There was nothing wrong with this newly-renovated bathroom—except that it was a real snooze. A new mirror, egg yolk yellow paint, and an accent wall gave it much-needed personality. Notice how guests will see the wallpaper and art when they look at themselves in the mirror.

right

Because this loft was a rental, we couldn't change everything! The kitchen was one place in particular where I had to pick and choose what was worth switching out. The tile already had yellow in it, so I decided to lean into that hue to make it feel more intentional. We were stuck with stainless accents, but my clients loved brass, so we broke "rules" and used both! I also added open shelves to the walls to increase storage and add some life to the dull drywall.

DAZEY DIY

Amend store-bought art. I loved this wire wall sculpture, but it was disappearing into the wallpaper, so I bought yellow yarn and tied on strips to create a fringe-y effect. Now it's a totally custom artwork!

Wallpapering this desk nook in the kitchen was a no-brainer: It turned a nothing space into a cute corner and balanced beautifully with the yellow accent wall opposite. Sunshine-y accessories complement the pattern.

Just one wall of gorgeous green wallpaper added so much depth to this space. While my personal preference is for a bright, adventurous sofa, these clients wanted a neutral sofa. When going quieter with furniture, I focus on shape, texture, and contrast. This couch appealed because of its interesting U shape, pillow back, and nice, nubby fabric. Then I added some pops of pink with the pillows and throw, and the couch itself pops against the dark green wallpaper.

The light fixture reminds me of a kinetic sculpture. I liked it so much, I ended up using a similar fixture in my own home (you can see it on page 33).

opposite

For the recording room, soft and sound-absorbing was the name of the game. Cue the Moroccan rugs and loads of lush velvet. This modular sofa was extra plush and adaptable, plus I could order pieces to fit the room's awkward shape, and they could move the ottoman around, as needed.

right

This corner is where my clients interview their guests. In addition to creating a cute space, I was concerned with the acoustics. To help improve their audio quality, I hung double curtain rods and two sets of thick velvet drapes, opted for upholstered swivel armchairs, and layered up cushy carpets.

NOT-AT-ALL-CORPORATE OFFICES

This co-working space and entrepreneur's workplace were designed to foster creativity.

You could probably guess that the offices I have designed don't look like the rest of corporate America. I started out my career with a traditional job in a conventional office where you sit at your desk all day long. Let me tell you: That is very uninspiring. Most workplaces are colorless, monotonous, and totally lacking in personality. If a company has made an effort to inject some color into their interiors, it's rarely done with any sense of play or personality.

My first time designing an office was partially an act of self-preservation: I'd just launched my fashion line and Phillip and I were living in a small apartment. I was trying to work out of coffee shops and rent-a-desk situations, but neither worked for me. I needed a dedicated place to work for hours at a time, but I also wanted a place with good backdrops for me to create content and non-desk areas to take little breaks. So, a friend and I ended up starting our own co-working space.

Our co-working space, which we dubbed Biz Babez (this was during the peak "girl boss" era), was very scrappy and done on a shoestring budget, but it was a huge learning experience about how offices can work better to serve creatives. It was also the first time I designed a public-facing space.

Since then, I've created several offices for clients, and I've discovered that a well-designed workplace doesn't just look good: It makes employees feel good to be there. This chapter lays out how I've made working spaces look more like a cool living room or a chic coffee shop.

CAFÉ-INSPIRED CO-WORKING

When I paid to be a member of a co-working space, I had a dedicated desk that I rented, but I never ended up using it. So, when we created our creative co-working space, I made the work zones more like the common areas I gravitated to.

above

These desks are actually display tables from a shop that was closing. Going-out-of-business sales are great places to get seriously discounted office furnishings.

right

This conference table setup is a reminder that the lines between office and home furniture aren't cut-and-dried: This wood table and midcentury-esque chairs work great for a big meeting, but could just as easily service a dinner party.

Hide an unsightly feature. The fiber artwork is a custom piece that I commissioned to cover a weird window that goes into another office. Make your own art to disguise ugly features like electrical panels.

I knew I wanted a majorly pink backdrop somewhere in the space, and I was thrilled when the landlord agreed to let us paint the biggest wall. I embraced the color with a pink sofa and accessories. This concentrated color creates a satisfying "moment" in a space that was a little bit of a hodgepodge because we were on a budget. You can do the same by painting a wall to match your sofa.

left

Even one wall of "wow" wallpaper can make an office feel more like a living room. I was so stoked to install this Justina Blakeney wallpaper that I had long admired. If you've had a wallpaper on your wish list for more than a year, it's a safe bet you'll like it a long time.

below

When my business partner and I were figuring out how to furnish the Biz Babez space, we connected with a fellow female entrepreneur, a vintage furniture dealer whose business was called Amsterdam Modern. She generously lent us some pieces from her warehouse with the understanding that anything in the space was for sale—so furniture could get swapped out at any time if someone bought it. Likewise, we found local artists who were excited to hang their art in our space for sale, kind of like how some coffee shops sell art.

opposite

This co-working space was where I discovered the power of a daybed: Everyone was obsessed with this spot. Sometimes you need not only a change of place, but a change in elevation while you are working.

left

Sometimes I forgo a mural in favor of simple painted shapes, like we did in the main workspace of this office. It's a great way to add a burst of color to the wall without having to paint the entire thing. Think of it as a mural-redux or a happy compromise between wallpaper and a fully painted wall.

below

The fronts of the stairs were originally painted black. To make them more fun and feminine, I covered them over with an abstract wallpaper that flows up the stairs. If you're patient and precise with an X-Acto knife, this is a project you can do yourself.

A FUN & FEMININE FOUNDRY

Your office should reflect your business's personality. Looking at these photos, you wouldn't be surprised that I designed this office for a female entrepreneur. She loves that girly-girly feeling, so I designed this custom mural for her and built the color scheme of pinks, coral, green, and sage from it. The curvy Mario Bellini sofa and blush-tinted ceiling reinforce the feminine theme.

above left

I painted the dining area adjacent to the kitchen with a split-wall effect to create a visual extension of the kitchen cabinets. My client already had this table, so I sourced pieces to complement it. When working with a mishmash of furnishings, getting the wood tones to match as closely as possible is key to a cohesive look.

above right

The space had no proper kitchen, so we had to build one. I wanted it to feel like an at-home cooking space. In addition to the basics, I designed a custom island built from terrazzo, added a fun backsplash, and changed all of the recessed lighting. A cheerful room like this helps employees enjoy their mini breaks throughout the day.

opposite bottom

Because it was a rented space, I was super limited in what I could do with the bathroom. So, we did a paint-only makeover. We hid the dated floor tile with black concrete paint. Then we created a faux trim paint line between color blocks on the wall and coated the ceiling in an off-black.

right

The previous tenant in this space was a hair salon, and my client was stuck with the capped pipes along this wall. To avoid pricey plumbing work, we built a plywood box around them and designed a banquette to go right on top. What had been a problem ended up leading to a cool design moment. Note how I used paint to camouflage the built-in cabinets in the wall too—sneaky!

NOT-AT-ALL-CORPORATE OFFICES
TIPS & TRICKS

Reflect your brand

Before you embark on an office design project, it's helpful to do a little brainstorming about what your brand is about. The decor should align with your mission and whatever service or product your company sells.

Don't buy only office furniture

With a few exceptions, I purchased very few official furnishings for the workplaces I have designed. Instead, I look for domestic furniture that can work in an office setting.

Channel the cool coffee shop

When designing a working space, think of your favorite café and design it more like that: Little bistro tables and comfortable armchairs—not cubicles!—are where people really want to work and take calls.

Charging is key

While I love a space to look homey, an office needs way more outlets than your average home. Plan for extra outlets in areas where people are likely to be working for longer periods.

Bring in the cute carpets

One of the fastest ways to make a boring office feel more like an arty apartment is to style it with some design-forward area rugs. Rugs also help soften the acoustics and can define rooms within rooms in an open plan.

Don't forget the details

Art and houseplants are the finishing touches that make an office feel less, well, office-y and more like a place you want to hang all day. If your business doesn't have a huge budget for decor, you could consider artists to do a gallery-style show in your space like we did in our co-working space.

When in doubt: paint

You can't always make big changes in an office rental, but you can usually paint. Color on the walls can go a long way toward making your workplace a more authentic expression of your business.

SPACES MADE TO SHOOT

These client projects were all contrived as content creation locations, and they are bursting with lessons for how to create a space that looks good both IRL and in 2-D.

As an entrepreneur and content creator, I've always designed my interiors with an eye for how they will appear in photographs, and my experience starting a clothing line has given me an inside perspective on what makes a great photoshoot location. Using my own homes as backdrops for my clothing line led several other creatives to hire me to help design their content-creation spaces, which I've gathered in this chapter.

Designing a space with content creation in mind might seem extreme, but if you're an entrepreneur of any kind, you're probably familiar with the feeling that you constantly need to be producing new images for your brand—whether that's podcasting, performing, fashion design, or even accounting. Having a thoughtfully designed space makes it so much easier to fulfill those demands.

When I design a space that will double as a location for image making, every little element needs to be something you could take a picture of—there are no wasted corners. This means the spaces in this chapter have more backdrops than you might normally see in a single space, but you can dial that back for your own interiors. Rooms created for photography or film are also a little bolder and more wildly colored than you might prefer in everyday life. (I am a maximalist, but in some of these projects, the client was pushing me to go more colorful!) The good news for you? Because these spaces were maximized for creating content, they are jam-packed with ideas you can borrow.

DAZEY DIY

Riff on a classic. My clients loved the iconic Ultrafragola Mirror by Ettore Sottsass, but it was outside of their budget. We had a custom mirror fabricated with a similar wavy edge to match their color palette.

AN OH-SO-SATURATED SHOOT LOCATION

When a fashion brand asked me to create a photo studio for their brand, they had a raw, empty room attached to their warehouse. What they wanted was a chromatic space where they could create content and invite influencers to see collections. To make it feel more inviting and to counteract the very industrial feel, I really leaned into bold colors and a lot of clever concealment.

There is A LOT going on in this space, with all the different backdrops, but I didn't want it to look totally crazy. You'll see shades of pink are used again and again to tie it all together; the wallpaper patterns are also relatively subdued to support the audacious palette.

DAZEY DIY

Create flattering lighting on a budget. I hung a bunch of simple globe lights at different heights for visual interest. Versatile milk-glass globes offer soft, diffused light and you can find them at any big box store.

opposite

To makeover the studio entrance, we added colorful adhesive glass film to the existing doors. This glass film is such a fun way to give a boring glass door extra personality.

right

When designing a photo studio, I think about creating vignettes— little rooms within a room. This tactic can also be helpful when designing a large, open-concept living space. In this studio we painted corrugated metal panels to define the vignettes (and conceal the rough walls).

DAZEY DIY

Make a rainbow. If you have a large wall of windows like this, consider drawing a rainbow with curtains. I found a simple velvet panel that was available in multiple hues and ordered one of each—so easy!

CONTENT CREATION WAREHOUSE

A pair of photographers hired me to create a vibrant photography studio that they could use themselves and rent out when they weren't using it. This was one of the very few projects where the clients were asking me to go more saturated with the colors.

above left

They say a photo is worth a thousand words; I say a good chair is worth a thousand photographs. Investing in a fun, statement chair, like this hanging acrylic bubble chair, creates an invitation to snap a photo—whether that's in a pro studio setting or at your next party.

above right

The wall murals here are based on the furnishings for a cool, radiating effect. For the mirror bullseye, I used a string compass to create the design, but for the portion of the graphic that plays off the sofa, I created the silhouette freehand.

left

Because we were on a tight budget, I looked for affordable ways to inject interest into the studio. One solution was to source a bunch of vintage pieces, including this quirky floor lamp and planter, and spray paint them in wild colors.

You can find such fun vintage art at thrift stores, but often the frames are kind of meh. My solution is to paint them a bright color that coordinates with the rest of the space. Since frames rarely get touched, they're unlikely to chip.

opposite

Here's another example of an affordable art DIY: I sourced thrift store paintings and completely covered them in paint. I taped some off to create a color-blocked effect and painted the smaller ones in solid hues. The resulting art looks great in the background of a photo.

NOT YOUR GRANDMA'S VICTORIAN

My creative client wanted to create a modern Victorian backdrop for her work, but how do you create a period-inspired fantasia in a totally bland, vanilla house? Of course, I used tons of patterns and color, but the first step was to add molding, a proper mantel, and other architectural details to the room. Molding really changes the way a room feels, even if you don't notice it immediately.

The Divine Savages wallpaper that graces the ceiling was the starting point for this room: I knew it would set the tone for the space with its punchy colors and very Victorian vibes. This brand knows you need to dial up the saturation on the color palette to make an older era of design feel of-the-moment.

left

Sometimes you just need to pick a material and go wild with it, like I did in this room with fringe. There's fringe in the curtains, the lights, the pillows, and even the chandelier. I chose to focus on fringe for its turn-of-the-century feel, but in these colors it looks new and fresh.

opposite

Ugly masonry can be intimidating, but I used stripes of cement paint to make the off-centered brick fireplace feel more balanced. And that super-fancy mantel? It's actually something I bought online that we just glued into place. Chaises and slipper chairs are great choices for spaces where you create content because it's easy for a model to display an outfit— and they're also great for parties.

This multiuse room veers a little further away from our Victorian inspiration, but relates to the other rooms with its matching ceiling rosette and blush color scheme. If you have a utilitarian space, it can still be a creative backdrop. For example, you can change in this dressing room, but you can also create content. We went super-girly with the lip motif supergraphic, but you could do something that relates to your niche, like a silhouette of a fruit in a kitchen or a tool in a workshop.

1 CEILING MEDALLION, 3 WAYS

How much do I love this ceiling medallion? Let me count the ways: It added so much charm and character to these detail-less, white-box rooms. Using the medallion in every room established a theme and commonality across a bold, varied design. Medallions are also one of the easiest things to DIY: You nail-gun it in place and then spackle the holes. Finally, it is so versatile, it looks just as great with a splurge Murano chandelier as with a cheap and cheerful tassel pendant.

opposite

Here's a fun way to play with patterns: Take one print and use it in multiple colorways in one room. If you look closely, you'll see that the ceiling, accent wall, and the paper within the moldings are all the same design in different colors.

right

The first thing you see when you look at this room is All. The. Color. But so much of the transformation is due to the ways we added details to the plain room: Crown molding, ceiling details, the chair rail, and the cool, premade panels with the wallpaper inside of them all give the room layers of interest.

THAT 70s SHOOT SPACE

Sometimes a room whispers what it wants to be; other times it shouts. This giant den with its original terrazzo floors and wood-paneled walls was calling out for a retro-inspired design. Luckily, my client agreed that a throwback theme would be a fun backdrop for photographs and videos.

opposite

There's power in repetition, which is why I sometimes bring in the same visual theme over and over. In this corner, you can see variations on the wavy motif in the carpet, supergraphic, and wallpaper.

left

I adored the den's untouched wood paneling, but leaving it alone would make it hard to achieve my signature Dazey style. So, I designed a supergraphic that paid no mind to the architecture: It goes right over the mantle, the fireplace, and onto the ceiling. That one gesture signals that this room is a cheeky homage to the past—not an actual time capsule.

right

Even though my style is maximalist, I prefer to keep surfaces clear and clutter to a minimum. So instead of relying on accessories to create a vibe, I emphasize the room's themes in functional elements like shaggy rugs, door curtains, and the sputnik-style light in the dining area.

opposite

This kitchen adjoins the retro den, but it had none of the throwback elements: It was simple and gray. Swapping out the plain appliances with the vintage-looking ones and adding '70s-style wallpaper made a big impact on the vibe. I also played with paint, color-blocking the existing cabinets with a graphic design.

right

Accessories can really help sway the style of a bland kitchen. Here, the vintage mixing bowls and other retro-looking pieces draw attention away from the boring choices the builder made. I especially love displaying curated finds on floating shelves like these.

SPACES MADE TO SHOOT
TIPS & TRICKS

One space, many backdrops

When you're designing a space to shoot, you need to treat each wall and corner as a possible backdrop. Then use some decorating device, like a color scheme or theme, to tie them together.

Take a photo

Whenever I am creating a space, and especially when I am designing a space for shoots, I use my phone to quickly frame up vignettes and see how it looks. A photo in the moment is always a great way to tell exactly what it's going to look like later on.

Stop the scroll

Something that I keep in mind with content creation spaces is, what will grab your attention when you're scrolling? Our attention spans are dwindling down to nothing these days, so you need a little bit more of an in-your-face aesthetic when you're designing a space to be shared on social media.

Err on the warm side

If I am designing a space for content creation, I tend not to use as many cool colors because they can cast an unflattering light on skin tones, whereas warm colors reflect a more flattering glow.

Pay attention to lighting

Warmth is also important in lighting. Good, even lighting is always important, but doubly so in rooms where you plan to take photographs and videos. I make sure these spaces have an option for really bright, warm lighting. Also: Dimmers are your friend!

Choose charismatic furniture

When you're shopping for your home, it's tempting to play it safe with neutral, "classic" furniture pieces, but I believe cool statement furniture—such as a sofa shaped like lips or a cloud—can be a great conversation starter and so key for creating compelling content.

Start with wallpaper

Wallpaper is often the main inspiration for the color scheme in rooms I'm designing to be used as shoot locations. Beginning with that one element and then creating the rest of the room around it is a foolproof way to make a space look polished.

RESOURCES

AKA: Just tell us where you got all the cute stuff, Dani!

ANTHROPOLOGIE

The fashion-to-home pipeline is real! I love to browse the home section at Anthropologie because their buyers curate such a beautiful mix of well-designed pieces—with lots of color!

www.anthropologie.com/house-home

BEND GOODS

A furniture maker based in Los Angeles that manufactures wire chairs, tables, wall art, and more, Bend Goods is a great place to shop for design-forward outdoor furniture.

www.bendgoods.com

BUSINESS & PLEASURE CO.

This is the source for the cutest outdoor umbrellas and furniture; everything they sell is full of color and makes you feel like you're at a fancy hotel.

www.businessandpleasureco.com

CHAIRISH

I consider Chairish to be my Goldilocks "just right" choice among secondhand e-commerce sites: Not too big, not too pricey. Chairish toes the line between the high-end 1stDibs and Etsy and eBay, where there is so much for sale, it's often hard to find the good stuff.

www.chairish.com

CONCRETE COLLABORATIVE

This California-based brand is my go-to source for concrete tiles, including the ones in My Dazey Desert House (see page 149). I am also hopelessly devoted to their drop-dead gorgeous terrazzo countertops. Plus, I like Concrete Collaborative's environmentally responsible manufacturing practices.

www.concrete-collaborative.com

DIVINE SAVAGES

This British home brand sells super-colorful classic wallpapers but done in a fresh and fun way. They also offer home accessories that coordinate with their wall patterns.

www.divinesavages.com

DROP IT MODERN

You'll find lots of funky abstract wallpapers and murals in great colors on this site. They also have customization options, like adjusting the color, size, and scale of any print.

www.dropitmodern.com

ETERNITY MODERN

This company custom makes classic midcentury silhouettes to your exact specifications. I've used them when the original item was beyond budget or unavailable in the colors or finishes I desired.

www.eternitymodern.com

ETSY

A marketplace for just about everything, I often use Etsy to commission one-of-a-kind pieces. If you're working with a specific color scheme and can't find a rug or a frame, there is almost always an Etsy maker who will customize something for you. You can also find good vintage pieces on the site.

www.etsy.com

FACEBOOK MARKETPLACE

For local secondhand deals, nothing beats Facebook Marketplace these days. I have found many great pieces, but you have to have patience (and transportation!) to score the gems.

www.facebook.com/marketplace

FIRECLAY TILE

For vibrant, handmade tile, you can't go wrong with Fireclay. They have so many options, and I love their sustainable business ethos.

www.fireclaytile.com

HAUSTILE

I used Haustile's modern, porcelain tile at the Trixie Motel (see page 196) and in my Alabama client's project (see page 70). I loved collaborating with this super-cool, female-owned brand on my own tile collection that has five unique patterns.

www.haustileco.com

HOUSE OF HACKNEY

The gorgeous and timeless maximalist prints from House of Hackney are available in an array of color options. I love that their wallpapers are really detailed and illustrative.

www.houseofhackney.com

HYGGE & WEST

This boutique wallpaper company has some of the prettiest patterns. I used their designs in My California Bungalow Gone Wild and My Dazey Desert House (see pages 30, 36, and 149). I also love that they offer shower curtains and bedding of many of their prints, so you can create a monoprint look.

www.hyggeandwest.com

INDUSTRY WEST

A furniture brand that has cool pieces that don't look like everyone else's, Industry West often offers interesting collaborations. I have a couple of pieces from their Contour Collection in my own home.

www.industrywest.com

JONATHAN ADLER

I've got a hunch Jonathan and I would get along famously. His happy-chic brand is one of my favorite sources for gorgeous, curated, fun pieces. Jonathan Adler is especially great for lighting and unique statement decor pieces.

www.jonathanadler.com

JOYBIRD

I was a Joybird customer long before I collaborated with them on my own collection. Joybird became my trusted source for affordable upholstered furniture because of their wide variety of fabrics and customization options.

www.joybird.com

KIP & CO

It's hard to find quality bedding with playful colors and prints, which is why I've used Australian brand Kip & Co in several of my projects. It's a bonus that they're still a little under the radar stateside.

www.kipandco.com

KOHLER

A trusted name for all things bath, I adore the fact that Kohler recently brought back some heritage colors for sinks and toilets.

www.kohler.com

MITZI

Finding lighting fixtures that are thoughtfully designed, well made, and not wildly expensive can be hard, but Mitzi consistently delivers killer designs at accessible price points.

www.mitzi.com

POPHAM DESIGN

For graphic, patterned concrete tile—think mod zigzags and arches—I often turn to Popham Design, a tile brand that is based in Marrakech, Morocco.

www.pophamdesign.com

REFORM

If you're looking for high-quality kitchen cabinets with a fresh modern look, Reform has you covered. I chose their Basis cabinets for My Dazey Desert House (see page 153) because of their 1960s-inspired design.

www.reformcph.com

SIGNATURE HARDWARE

For kitchen hardware, I often choose Signature Hardware: They make really beautiful brass faucets, and I've used their dope brass sink in a lot of projects.

www.signaturehardware.com

SPOONFLOWER

Spoonflower is my go-to destination for unique patterns. Not only did Spooflower let me create my own collection (a dream come true!), but they support thousands of other small businesses, artists, and designers with their on-demand printing processes for fabric, wallpaper, bedding, and more.

www.spoonflower.com

TOTAL DESIGN FURNITURE

This amazing, California-based fabricator created all the custom furniture for Trixie Motel (see page 165), and I've used them for client projects as well. If you can dream it, they can build it.

www.totaldesign.co

TOV FURNITURE

Tov makes quirky, fun, and colorful statement furniture at a great price, like the cute desk in my "cloffice" (see page 136). I love their motto: "Don't be boring."

www.tovfurniture.com

ACKNOWLEDGMENTS

My name may be on the cover, but this book belongs to my husband, Phillip Butler, as much as it does to me. Phillip has been working behind the scenes on Dazey Designs and the Dazey Den since the very beginning, and Phillip has believed in my dreams even more than I did myself at times. Thank you for everything, Phillip; I am so lucky to have you by my side in both life and work.

Thank you also to my parents, Cristina and Holger, who saw an artistic spark in me at a young age and fostered it. I'm so grateful you always encouraged me in every creative endeavor, and I wouldn't have this bold, happy, creative career without you cheering me on.

I am so grateful to the team who brought this book to life. Thank you especially to my editor, Juliet Dore, who had a vision for what this book could be. Thanks to my cowriter, Laura Fenton; designers Danielle Youngsmith and Heesang Lee; and Annalea Manalili and the rest of the team at Abrams. To my manager, Ali Wald, thank you for championing me in this and all endeavors.

Finally, thank you to all of my clients who entrusted me with bringing their interior dreams to life. This book is yours too.

ABOUT THE AUTHOR

DANI DAZEY is a fashion, print, and interior designer known for her joyful, maximalist style. After a career working for large fashion brands, Dani founded her own clothing line, Dazey LA, in 2016. Sharing her work on social media, Dani found an audience hungry for her bold, colorful approach to life. Drawing on her knowledge of trends, color, and textiles, Dani branched out to pursue her passion for interior decorating as well. Dani's interior design work gained wide recognition, including features in many publications, such as *Architectural Digest*, *Domino*, *Dwell*, and *The Jungalow*, among others. When Dani was cast as the designer on the reality remodeling show *Trixie Motel*, alongside drag queen Trixie Mattel, the show introduced her signature Dazey interiors to an even wider audience. Today, Dani is focused fully on interior design and her home products, leaving fashion behind for now. Dani wrote *The Maximalist* to empower even more people to be daring with their decor and express themselves to the fullest.

www.dazeyden.com
@danidazey

Editor: Juliet Dore
Designer: Heesang Lee
Design Manager: Danielle Youngsmith
Managing Editor: Annalea Manalili
Production Manager: Larry Pekarek

Library of Congress Control Number: 2024943647

ISBN: 978-1-4197-7650-2
eISBN: 979-8-88707-387-3

Printed and bound in China
10 9 8 7 6 5 4 3 2 1

Abrams books are available at special discounts when purchased in quantity
for premiums and promotions as well as fundraising or educational use. Special
editions can also be created to specification. For details, contact
specialsales@abramsbooks.com or the address below.

Abrams® is a registered trademark of Harry N. Abrams, Inc.

ABRAMS The Art of Books
195 Broadway, New York, NY 10007
abramsbooks.com